JOHN F. DEDEK was born in Chicago in 1929 and attended Saint Mary of the Lake Seminary in Mundelein, Illinois, where he received his doctorate in sacred theology in 1958. Father Dedek served as associate pastor of St. Gilbert Church in Grayslake, Illinois, from 1958 to 1965. He is currently Professor of Moral Theology at Saint Mary of the Lake Seminary and associate editor of **Chicago Studies.** Father Dedek is the author of **Experimental Knowledge of the Indwelling Trinity** and of numerous articles in **Theological Studies, The American Ecclesiastical Review, The New Catholic Encyclopedia** and elsewhere.

Contemporary
Sexual Morality

Contemporary Sexual Morality

by John F. Dedek

SHEED and WARD   New York

© Sheed and Ward, Inc., 1971
Library of Congress Catalog Card Number: 79-152319
Standard Book Number: 8362-1159-6

Portions of this book originally appeared in
Chicago Studies and are reprinted by permission of the publisher.

Manufactured in the United States of America

Contents

Foreword

IT IS a commonplace to say that we live in a rapidly changing world. What is not so common is the realization that in a changing world man's own self-image will change profoundly. It is easy to overstate and even caricature these nuances in self-image. I believe that John Macquarrie has succeeded eminently in avoiding this danger. In *Three Issues in Ethics* he lists as the five most striking characteristics of contemporary man's self-understanding the following: an awareness of himself as a being-on-the-way, a changing being; a sharper realization of himself as embodied, a being-in-the-world; a renewed grasp of himself as essentially social, a being-with-others; man as agent, not merely thinker; and man as responsible. The Second Vatican Council, in its great document on the Church in the Modern World, showed itself highly sensitive to these resonances, so much so that at times it appears to have forgotten that man was, is and always will be sinful man.

What at least very many in the Catholic community fail to realize is that a shift in self-image as radical as that which characterizes the "new man" is bound to affect theology at all levels. For theology is dominantly concerned with an understanding of God's dealing with man. When man's own anthropological premises shift, his theology—to the extent that it is alive and well—will necessarily reflect and record these shifts. To the outsider this may appear to be a type of effete faddism, to coin a phrase. To the theologian it is the dead serious and often uneven struggle to reformulate the *magnalia Dei* in a more meaningful way.

There has been a very special resistance to this idea in the area of Christian morals, probably because the investment in moral concepts and convictions is so utterly personal. Nevertheless, when theological ethicists begin to assimilate into their procedural methods the full impact of man's new self-image, things are going to happen both to moral science and to moral scientists. The science itself will be stamped with a new mood. James Gustafson has rightly—give or take a phrase or two—characterized this mood with a series of contrasts: dynamic vs. static, open vs. closed, future-looking vs. an orientation to the past, creative responsibility vs. conformity to a predefined order, visceral morality vs. cerebral morality and so on. The moral theologian himself will reflect this mood in his own tentativeness, openness, sensitivity to history, humility and willingness to listen, learn and change when change is appropriate.

John Dedek's reflections on human sexuality are a refraction of some of these larger stirrings. Dedek wisely settles for the fact that human sexuality is going to remain a *mysterium tremendum*. Hence his essays are not in-depth explorations controlled by a single, dazzlingly profound and utterly original insight. They are rather kaleidoscopic overviews of some practical problems and the state of discussion (particularly in Catholic circles) surrounding them. As such they are more like a very useful report to the community on the direction things can be expected to take. They reveal a man who has reflected honestly and openly, is respectful of tradition without being enslaved by it, is proportionately tentative and speaks directly and candidly.

Since the views of my friend and colleague Josef Fuchs, S.J., and myself are the occasion of so much of Dedek's comment, it must be said that in many instances these views have changed substantially while Dedek was putting his study together. But that is the way it is these days with that small fraternity that plies the troubled but exciting waters of Christian morals. The classroom is no longer aptly symbolized by the dogmatic dais, but by the laboratory where a practitioner can float his ideas, test and reassess them and in general come out of the corner admitting nothing worse than an honest mistake. Dedek's essays reflect this spirit. In other words, in contemporary moral writings, we have the right to expect not the last word, but only a thoughtful word. That is what we get here from Dedek.

RICHARD A. McCORMICK, S.J.
*President, Catholic
Theological Society of America*

Contemporary
Sexual Morality

1. The Human Sexual Experience

BEFORE ATTEMPTING any theological reflections, ethical evaluations or practical conclusions in the area of human sexuality, it will be useful to have a clear understanding of the phenomena. What we are after is not the highly technical information possessed by gynecologists but the kind of clear practical knowledge that is acquired through reading and experience by sophisticated and reflective husbands and wives. Here as everywhere else experience is the best teacher. The following limerick is popular today, but a bit optimistic:

> The word has come down from the dean
> That with the aid of the teaching machine
> King Oedipus Rex
> Could have learned about sex
> Without ever touching the queen.

But if experience is the best teacher, it is not the only one, nor is it generally adequate in itself. The studies of Kinsey, Masters and Johnson and others provide sufficient data to give a fairly accurate description of the sexual person in operation. The sexual function is as important a part of the phenomena as the sexual apparatus, and an understanding of the human sexual response will be a useful underpinning for our theological and ethical reflections.

Useful or necessary as this information is, it is not the most significant element in human sexuality, let alone the whole of it. The truly significant elements of *human* sexuality are psychological and interpersonal. Bereft of these distinctively human elements sexuality becomes banal, empty, trivial. This is the central thesis of Rollo May in his latest book, *Love and Will*.[1]

May's premise is that the neurotic, like the artist, is predictive of a society's future. Neurotics, like artists, have special antennae; they are sensitive to what exists in the unconscious depths of society and in another generation will appear on the phenomenological social level. For example, Freud found a striking number of sexual problems in his patients before World War I, although the Victorian society of his time repressed and denied these problems and even the words that described them; but after World War II these problems and the language describing them had spread throughout our whole society. During the 1930s psychiatrists found an abnormal amount of hostility in their neurotic patients; this burst on Western society in the violence of World War II. Anxiety was the central problem of neurotics in the forties, only to become a problem widely experienced and discussed in the fifties. One of the problems that especially troubled neurotic patients in the late forties and early fifties was the problem of identity, and this is a general problem in society today.

If this pattern holds, May argues, then the neurosis of today will become the "sociosis" of tomorrow: the principal problem being brought to psychiatrists today by patients undergoing therapy will affect society in general in the near future. And what is the chief problem of people in therapy today? It is, says May, an incapacity to love or will. The opposite of love is not hate but lack of feeling, lack of affect, *apátheia;* and the opposite of will is not indecisiveness (which may be an effort to decide) but being uninvolved, detached, unrelated personally to any significant event.

Modern technology, the mass media, the population explosion and other forces in society result in an individual's sense of anxiety and powerlessness, which in turn leads to despair, futility and emptiness. Bowed by the feeling that it is all *de trop,* the individual believes that he cannot significantly affect anything or anyone. He therefore tries to protect himself with the thought that it does not really matter anyway, that he does not really care, in fact *can* not really care about anyone or anything. One last desperate effort to prove that he can make a difference, that he can affect someone or something, is the violence that occurred in our society during the sixties. But the usual upshot is not violence but estrangement, playing it cool, alienation, apathy, a distance from persons and objects that used to excite one's affections and will.

The consequence of this, May says, is sex separated from eros, sex which becomes mechanical, without passion or commitment, without feeling or meaning. Our society today is obsessed with sexual talk and sexual activity. There are sexual opportunities of every sort for everyone, and yet the most frequently heard complaint in the offices of psychiatrists and marriage counselors is that there is in sex no feeling and therefore no fun. Was not that the very point of the movie *Alfie*? After years of sexual promiscuity, his burning question was about meaning.

Mechanical or depersonalized sex, May points out, is reflected in our language. *Fuck* is a good English word for expressing the release of sexual tension involved in an animal act. It describes what occurs on the purely biological level. But men do not only fuck, they also make love. And *making love* is not merely a euphemism for *fucking*. It describes a different kind of human experience. One may "have sex" or "make love." He may "screw" or "have intercourse." He may "lay" someone or "go to bed." But all these expressions do not mean the same thing. An act of personal intimacy is one thing. Biological sex without passion or feeling or caring is quite another.

Rollo May's observations form a useful context for our description of the physical, biological and mechanical aspects of human sexuality. The most significant elements of human sexuality are psychological and interpersonal, and only these elements give meaning to the physical.

SEXUAL ACTUATION

The differences in erotic stimulation between the two sexes are often exaggerated. In fact, the personal differences between members of the same sex are often greater than the average differences between the sexes in general. For instance, burlesque shows with female strippers, stag films and girlie magazines may seem to be of exclusively male interest; yet Kinsey reports that one-third of the females interviewed have as strong a sexual response to such stimuli as men and some an even stronger response.[2]

It seems altogether possible that the greatest difference between the sexes is determined by culture and education not by physical anatomy and hormones. From the earliest years children are taught to be different and how to be different. Girls are given dolls to play with and boys are given mechanical toys. They are dressed differently and are encouraged and expected to behave differently. Girls may cry, but boys are taught that crying is unmanly. Boys are asked by relatives what they are going to be when they grow up, while little girls are complimented on being pretty.

Rollo May confirms this view of our bisexuality when he reports a phenomenon that occurs when the sexes are separated:

> I once spent a week on Mt. Athos, a little country in northern Greece extending 12 miles into the Aegean Sea and populated only by monks living in fifteen or twenty monasteries. No woman, supposedly, had stepped off the boat at Athos since the twelfth century. But the monks themselves had taken on the gestures, the ways of talking, walking, and carrying themselves of women. I would find myself thinking, as I saw a monk walking away from me down the village street, that there was a *woman*. The same was true of

another very different masculine group, the Foreign Legion, the soldiers of which would dance with each other on the decks of the French ships in the Mediterranean. The incidence of homosexuality is not the point here and, in any case, does not explain the phenomenon. I propose, rather, that when there are no women present, there is no accent on acting male and vice versa; we become more masculine when there are women around, and they more feminine. *The two sexes have the function of accentuating the characteristics of the opposite sex.*[3]

Our sexuality is not primarily a biological condition given at birth but a condition in process, developing in interaction with cultural forces and the opposite sex. Men define their own maleness in interaction with females and vice versa, under the guidance and direction of the norms, mores and expectations of their culture. It is an oversimplification, therefore, to say that men are strong and women weak, men logical and women emotional, men aggressive and women passive.

Is not this what young people are telling us today? Young men no longer feel that it is unmanly to be emotional, gentle or soft and women are asking to be treated as equals with men. Men's hair is being worn as long as women's and many young women are using few if any cosmetics. Differences in dress are not as pronounced as before: women wear slacks and pants and men clothing which ten years ago would have been considered a sign of effeminacy. There are forces at work in our culture today that are assimilating the sexes. The artificial, arbitrary distinctions of the past are being discarded.

There are some differences in sexual arousal, at least presumptively. The presumption may have to yield to the fact in some instances, but some general statements are possible and useful.[4]

Both men and women respond to psychological seductiveness, but women more so than men. Verbal endearments, glances, courtesy, kindness, gentleness and sensitivity are very seductive and often necessary for any sexual response. Pace in sex play is also important to both sexes, especially again to women. Teasing, with advances and retreats, is important as technique in sexual arousal, and abandonment in the end is a most significant psychic factor. Variety also has an important role to play. As McCary notes, a wife who surprises her husband occasionally by slithering into his study wearing nothing but two very dry martinis and a smile can help prevent their sexual life from growing stale. Variety in sexual foreplay and positions in intercourse can be a valuable psychological stimulant. Timing is also important: generally, at least for the woman's sake, fifteen minutes of foreplay should precede coitus, although too long a time at foreplay can be counterproductive.

Among the physical factors relating to sexual arousal, bodily cleanliness is not only next to godliness, it is also nearer to the successful achievement of orgasm. Perhaps this should go without saying, but it is often overlooked. Even the faint smell or appearance of urine or fecal matter around the perineum can be unromantic.

One difference between men and women is that men respond more readily to visual stimulations and fantasy, although women are more easily stimulated by reading sexy romantic novels. The fact that sight is more stimulating to men than to women probably accounts for the fact that men are more often the aggressors in sexual activity. Motivated by what they see, they move to initiate more proximate contacts. Women, however, are the more tactile of the sexes. They respond sexually to touch to a greater degree than men do, not in the sense that they respond more quickly (in fact they generally require a longer period of foreplay than men), but in the sense that their entire skin is more erogenous.

The older moralists used to sort out the erogenous zones in the human body in terms of *partes inhonestae* (the evil parts of the body) and *partes minus honestae* (the less good parts of the body). The *partes inhonestae* were the genitalia; the *partes minus honestae* included the female breasts, upper arms and thighs and perhaps a few other locations, depending on the strictness of the author. Thanks to the sociological studies of Kinsey and the clinical studies of Masters and Johnson, we know that many other parts of the body, particularly of the female body, respond sexually to tactile stimulation.

The palm of a girl's hand is very responsive to touch and especially to kissing. So is the bend of her elbow, the inner side of her upper arms and the outer side of her thighs. That is why women like to hold hands, walk arm in arm or walk close together with thighs brushing. Their hair line, especially along the back of the neck, is very sensitive. So are the lobes of their ears, particularly the dimple behind their ears. Perhaps the reason they put perfume behind their ears is to attract men to that spot.

One of the most erogenous zones is the mouth, lips and nose. Kissing is usually more erotic for women than men, although men also generally find it stimulating. In both sexes there is a great concentration of nerve endings there. Most people find "French" or "soul" or "deep" kissing very erotic. This kind of kissing is moist, with mouths open, and includes the gentle nipping of the inner lips and slight pressure with an exploring and darting tongue on the inner side of the lips and teeth. Rarely does it ever include any deep penetration by the tongue into the mouth of the other.

Because the mouth and lips are so erogenous,

it is not surprising that oral-genital contact is so popular, at least among more sophisticated people. Kinsey reports that 60% of the people who have gone to college experience oral-genital contacts, while only 20% of those who have gone to high school and 10% of those who have gone to grade school engage in this practice. When a man licks the genitalia of a woman the act is called "cunnilingus" (which comes from two Latin words meaning "licking the cunt"), and when a woman kisses, licks and sucks a man's penis her act is called "fellatio" (which is Latin for "sucking"). Many couples find it useful to engage in mutual oral-genital contact during the early part of stimulation as they are preparing for coitus.

Another highly erogenous zone in women is the breasts, especially the nipples and the areolae. They are not as erogenous, however, as most men suppose. Only 50% of women seem to find the fondling of their breasts very stimulating, whereas 75% of the men are themselves stimulated by fondling a female breast. Moreover, since there are only a certain number of nerve endings in every female breast, these are more diffused in larger breasts and more concentrated in smaller breasts. Smaller breasts, like Audrey Hepburn's or Twiggy's, are considerably more erogenous than larger ones, like Raquel Welch's or Ann-Margret's. The best technique to bring about sexual arousal is to massage the breast gently with a light brushing of the nipple and an occasional tweak at its sensitive tip, plus moist kisses with wet lips and an exploring tongue.

A woman's hips, abdomen, inner sides of the thigh, perineum and anus also are very responsive to stimulation. Most erogenous of all, of course, are the genitals, especially the labia minora, vestibule and above all the clitoris. Except for the upper front area, the vagina has very few nerve endings and is somewhat insensitive. The cervix is so insensitive that it can be surgically cut without anesthesia.

In men the erogenous zones are more localized. Most erogenous of all is the glans penis, particularly the lower surface at the corona and frenum. The skin on the shaft is not very sensitive, although gentle stroking or grasping of it and the scrotum is generally useful to a girl trying to excite a male. The male's nipples and areolae are also erogenous. Gentle rolling of the nipple between the thumb and forefinger and oral contact can be very stimulating.

From the descriptions above one can see that the term *erogenous zone* is not univocal. Sometimes it refers to those areas whose touch or fondling leads to sexual excitement. In a more restricted sense it designates those areas which become tumescent, which swell because they become engorged with blood during sexual stimulation: the penis, the clitoris, the labia minora, the nipples and areolae.

As is not so well known, the ear lobes and the inner nose also often become tumescent through sexual stimulation. The heavy breathing that occurs during sexual excitement is not only due to an increase in the rate of respiration but also to the occlusion of the air passageways in the nose because of the tumescence of the inner lining. There is some connection of the nose with sexuality that is not understood scientifically. It has been clinically observed that many people sneeze when becoming sexually aroused, and some women bleed sympathetically from the nose during their menstrual periods. Perhaps the connection is somehow vestigial: the sexual contacts of many animals include a considerable amount of sniffing.

Although many contemporary marriage manuals treat at great length the various positions that are possible in coitus, most of the information on their pages is of no great practical value to anyone. The detailed descriptions may serve the reader's prurient interest or suggest some possibilities to those who are especially athletic or acrobatic. Obviously, a couple should assume whatever position they find most comfortable and pleasurable and be willing to experiment occasionally for the sake of variety.

Basically there are four possible positions, each of which has its advantages and disadvantages. The most common position in Western culture is face to face with the man on top of the woman. The advantages of this position are that the man has the initiative, it is easy for him to make and maintain contact even after orgasm and his strong pelvic thrusts are accentuated. The disadvantages are that the woman's active and imaginative part is restricted, penetration for some couples is too deep, there is often little contact with the clitoris and the position is uncomfortable for a woman whose husband is too heavy.

The face-to-face position with the woman on top of the man provides more control for the woman and allows her to regulate the depth of penile penetration and the force of the man's pelvic thrust. The man is more relaxed and so can more easily delay orgasm. His hands are left free to fondle the woman's breasts or to manipulate her clitoris.

When face to face and side by side both the man and the woman have more control and more freedom of arm movement. However, there is less pressure on the vulval area and the man's pelvic thrusts are felt as less vigorous.

Entering the vagina from the rear is more comfortable under certain circumstances, for instance in the advanced months of pregnancy. But it prevents face-to-face intimacy.

The physical reactions leading up to and attendant upon orgasm have been clinically observed by Dr. Masters and Mrs. Johnson, and their detailed findings have recently been published in their book

Human Sexual Response.[5] Briefly, what happens is this.

The female breasts enlarge about 20 to 25%. The areolae swell and the nipples erect. Sixty percent of men also experience an erection of their nipples. A vascular flush of the skin begins around the stomach and gradually spreads over most of the body in 75% of women and in 25% of men. In both sexes muscles throughout the body tense and begin involuntary movements and contractions. The rate of respiration increases, the number of heart beats per minute doubles and the blood pressure rises significantly.

In a woman who has had no children the labia majora thin, flatten and flare out; in women who have had children the labia majora become engorged and enlarge to two or three times their normal dimensions. The man's homologous organ, the scrotum, contracts and elevates the testes.

The woman's clitoris increases in size to almost one inch and appears to retract because the attendant labia minora enlarge to two or three times their normal size and deepen in color. The vagina begins "sweating" a lubricating fluid for the vaginal wall. Its inner two-thirds increases in size by 25%. At orgasm the vagina contracts three or four times (sometimes up to fifteen times). The uterus also contracts rapidly and irregularly at orgasm.

The man's penis stiffens and enlarges to about

six inches in length. The glans deepens in color but remains relatively soft at the top. Immediately before ejaculation the Cowper's glands secrete two or three drops of fluid. Then contractions of the urethra and the muscles at the base of the penis and around the anus produce an ejaculation of semen in four to eight spurts over a period of about three to ten seconds. The normal ejaculation would fill a teaspoon. The force of the ejaculation varies with individuals. Sometimes it simply oozes out and sometimes it is projected with a force that would carry it three feet or more. Usually it is projected with a force that would carry it about three inches.

As I mentioned above, all this is not what human sexuality is mainly about. Sexuality is a much more important, significant and powerful force in human life than any description of the merely biological elements could ever suggest. As Rollo May says, "Trivialize sex . . . as we will, or defend ourselves from its power by cynicism and playing it cool as we wish, sexual passion remains ready at any moment to catch us off guard and prove that it is still the *mysterium tremendum*."[6] What is involved in this mystery we will have occasion to consider in the chapters that follow.

2. Premarital Petting and Coitus

UNTIL RECENTLY, persuasive motives for premarital chastity were easily found. The more obvious motives, which many young people found sufficiently convincing, are noted in the following limerick:

> There was a young lady named Wilde
> Who kept herself quite undefiled
> By thinking of Jesus
> And social diseases
> And the fear of having a child.

The motivation was both religious and pragmatic. Premarital sexual intimacy was forbidden by God and so was generally disapproved in Christian society. In addition, it exposed one to the danger of contracting one of the dreaded venereal diseases, such as gonorrhea or syphilis. They were painful, not

Contemporary Sexual Morality

easily cured and often resulted in serious complications and death. There also was the risk of pregnancy outside of marriage and the social stigma and economic loss which that involved.

Today these motives are losing their force. The religious motivation, "thinking of Jesus," no longer has the same generally persuasive power. A recent survey of the attitudes and behavior of college students conducted by Vance Packard and reported in his book *The Sexual Wilderness* shows that while students at two religiously affiliated colleges were somewhat more conservative, on the whole young people are no longer motivated by fear of sin or anxiety over guilt.[1] At the same time the Christian churches are tending to take a softer line in the whole area of premarital sex. More and more clergymen feel that religion should be accepting not judgmental and that preaching on sin or hell only serves to make people feel guilty, which of course no one should ever be made to feel.

Before the development of the "miracle drugs" in 1943 venereal diseases presented a serious threat. Now, if they are not prevented by prophylactic measures, they can easily be cured by antibiotics like penicillin. And to those who used to be worried about pregnancy one can say, with John Updike, "Welcome to the post-pill paradise."

PREMARITAL BEHAVIOR

One does not have to be a professional zoologist to know that infrahuman animals do not wait for marriage but begin to copulate with one another as soon as they are physically prepared. But what may not be so well known is that infrahuman animals also engage in a great amount of petting.[2] Since they lack man's prehensile hands, their techniques are less sophisticated. But it is an easily observable phenomenon that most mammals, when sexually aroused, crowd together, nuzzle, sniff, lick and touch each other's bodies. They kiss, lip to lip, tongue to tongue and mouth to genitals, and they often mount each other repeatedly without any effort at coitus. Like men, the male is usually the initiator and aggressor in this activity, and at least the male and perhaps also the female sometimes reach orgasm in the process.

Kinsey, who is a zoologist, notes that petting is a common phenomenon among cattle, horses, hogs, sheep, cats, lions, dogs, raccoon, rats, mice, guinea pigs, rabbits, skunks, monkeys, chimpanzees, porcupines and many other species.[3] Kinsey's conclusion was that at least in a biologic sense petting is normal and natural behavior.

To avoid confusion in terminology we can accept Kinsey's definition of petting as any physical contact short of coitus (i.e., short of the union of genitalia) which is used to provide sexual stimulation. Distinctions often drawn by young people among kissing, necking, light petting, heavy petting, petting above the waist, petting below the waist and so on merely describe differences in techniques and in the limits to which it is carried. For our purposes we will make the substantive distinction that everything from hand-holding and lip-kissing to oral-genital contacts and the apposition of genitalia which provides sexual stimulation, whether it proceeds to orgasm or not, can be called petting, since these actions do not involve the joining of the genitalia in the act properly called coitus.

Because of the wide range of individual differences and the difficulty many people had in recalling with accuracy their past sexual experiences, we do not get as clear a picture as we might hope for from the reports of Dr. Kinsey. He does tell us that by the age of fifteen 57% of the total male population in our country have had some petting experience; by the age of eighteen 84% and by the age of twenty-five 89%. Of these, one-third have petted to orgasm on the average of three to five times a week.

There is a direct correlation between education and petting: the more education, the more petting and the more intense the petting is. Of those who pet almost all engage in kissing; 55% (those with less education) to 87% (those with a college education) practice deep kissing; 78% to 99% fondle women's breasts; 36% to 93% manipulate their breasts orally; 79% to 92% fondle the genitals; and 9% to 18% engage in oral-genital contacts (cunnilingus and fellatio) before marriage. One-fourth have five or fewer partners and over one-third have twenty-one or more before they marry.

All these statistics still leave the picture of the actual situation somewhat blurred. By the age of twenty-five 85% of our male population have had some petting experience. But "some petting experience" is not especially illuminating. It could refer to a single kiss or hand-holding experience on one or a few occasions or to frequent, intense and promiscuous erotic behavior. We are told that of those who have had some petting experience one-third pet to orgasm with a frequency of three to five times a week. This means that by the age of twenty-five 10% of American men have not petted at all and 60% have petted to a point short of orgasm. What remains unclear is how many of this 60% pet habitually or with any regularity, how many pet infrequently and how many find petting a rare and isolated experience. Kinsey says that it is not easy to answer these questions because of the difficulty people had in trying to recall the frequency of these lesser sexual experiences. All he was able to conclude is that there is a great variety: some men pet every night and sometimes during the day as well while others go for months or years between petting experiences.

Kinsey's study of the petting practices of American girls provides the same kind of useful but blurred picture. Ninety percent of American females have had some petting experience in the wide sense of that phrase. By the age of fifteen 40% (as compared with 57% of the males) have petted; by the age of eighteen 69% to 95%, depending on their level of education (as compared with about 84% of the males) have petted; and by the age of twenty-five 88% of the female population (as compared with 89% of the men) have had some petting experience. It is interesting to note that only 80% of the women report that they have been erotically aroused by these experiences and that 31% pet to orgasm on the average of four to six times a year (as contrasted with one-third of the men who pet to orgasm three to five times a week). Ten percent of the women have had only one partner; 33% have had ten or more; and 19% have had twenty-one or more partners before marriage.

When we dig ourselves out of Kinsey's mountain of figures, we find some significant questions left unanswered. Of the 70% of American women who have not petted to orgasm, how many engage in regular intense petting and how many only in kissing or the light sort of petting that goes on publicly at cocktail parties and dances, and how many have petted only rarely or infrequently? Again, Kinsey says that it was very difficult for people to estimate the frequency of these less intense sexual experiences, especially since there were often long intervals between them.

Kinsey's interviews about premarital coitus revealed that among American men 98% of those who attended only grade school, 84% of those who attended high school and 67% of those who attended college have experienced coition before marriage. Here, unlike petting, there is an inverse relation between education and premarital intercourse: the more education, the less intercourse a man has.

Fifty percent of the women interviewed had premarital coitus, and of these one-half experienced it only with the man they eventually married. With the women the correlation between premarital coitus and education is just the opposite of that of the men: 30% with a grade school education, 47% with a high school education and 60% with a college education had sexual intercourse before marriage. One explanation for this is that those girls with less education married earlier, so that most of their teen-age coition could not be classified as premarital. Unmarried girls over twenty have about the same amount of sexual intercourse regardless of education. Here, as in the matter of petting, there is no way to ascertain whether those who have had premarital intercourse have had it regularly, frequently, seldom or only once.

Kinsey's studies were made around 1950, and many of the young people he interviewed are now grandparents. Therefore one might wonder about the validity of his studies today. Anyone who reads the newspapers, goes to movies or talks to young people in the seventies might reasonably suspect that the sexual behavior of the present generation is considerably more liberal than that of twenty years ago. What recent studies we have indicate just the opposite. Vance Packard's survey, made in 1967 and published in 1968, reveals that 58% of college men and 43% of college women have had premarital coitus (whereas according to Kinsey's study 67% of college men and 60% of college women had experienced premarital coition). Other recent studies reveal that while 75% of college girls think that their classmates are sleeping around, only about 20% have themselves had premarital intercourse.

Perhaps the most realistic conclusion that can be drawn from this is that the sexual revolution one hears so much about today is more talk than action. To say this is not to say that there is no revolution; much less is it to say that there is no problem. Rather, it locates the problem more exactly. While there has been no significant change in premarita

sexual behavior since the sexual revolution that occurred immediately after World War I, there has
been a shift in sexual attitudes. There is at present
a new revolution in the talking stage. An honest and
sincere conversation is going on among young people today and anyone with more than clichés to
offer can join in this conversation and perhaps con-
tribute to its eventual outcome.

SACRED SCRIPTURE

The Old Testament contains no general pro-
scription of premarital coitus. This is not surprising,
since even polygamy was tolerated. Deuteronomy
22:1–29 is sometimes offered as an instance of an
Old Testament condemnation of premarital coitus.
But a careful reading shows that what is in fact condemned here is (1) a woman deceiving her husband
before marriage into thinking that she is a virgin
when she is not, (2) rape and (3) sleeping with a
woman already betrothed to another man. Premarital coitus between two free and consenting persons
is not mentioned. Deuteronomy 23:17–19 and Ec-
clesiasticus 9:6 forbid sexual commerce with whores.
But prostitution cannot be simply equated with
sexual intimacy between an unmarried boy and girl.
The New Testament frequently condemns *por-*

Contemporary Sexual Morality

neia. But it is not clear that this word ever designates simple fornication. Its exact sense has to be derived from the immediate context. Sometimes it means adultery, as in Matthew 5:32 and 19:9, or incest, as in 1 Corinthians 5:1, or prostitution, as in 1 Corinthians 6:12–20. But that the New Testament ever forbids all sexual relations outside of marriage is not at all clear.

In 1 Corinthians 6:13–20 St. Paul writes:

> But the body—this is not meant for fornication; it is for the Lord, and the Lord for the body. God, who raised the Lord from the dead, will by his power raise us up too. You know, surely, that your bodies are members making up the body of Christ; do you think I can take parts of Christ's body and join them to the body of a prostitute? Never! As you know, a man who goes with a prostitute is one body with her, since *the two,* as it is said, *become one flesh.* But anyone who is joined to the Lord is one spirit with him. Keep away from fornication. All the other sins are committed outside the body; but to fornicate is to sin against your own body. Your body, you know, is the temple of the Holy Spirit, who is in you since you received him from God. You are not your own property; you have been bought and paid for. That is why you should use your body for the glory of God.

In this passage St. Paul is arguing against the libertine or antinomian converts among the Corin-

thians. They claimed that fornication was as necessary for the body as food and drink. It is clear that
the question being discussed by St. Paul is that of
sexual promiscuity with prostitutes. It is certainly
going beyond the text to say that Paul is condemning
all premarital sexual intercourse, even, for instance,
that between engaged couples.

The same ambiguity is found in 1 Thessalonians 4:3–4: "What God wants is for you all to be
holy. He wants you to keep away from fornication,
and each one of you to know how to use the body
that belongs to him in a way that is holy and honorable, not giving way to selfish lust like *the pagans
who do not know God*." The editor of the Jerusalem
Bible marks this passage as parallel to 1 Corinthians
6:13–20, which we have just exegeted. In his gloss
on this text in the *Jerome Biblical Commentary*
Joseph Fitzmyer indicates that sexual promiscuity is
probably the meaning of *porneia* here, since the pagan society that St. Paul refers to considered such
promiscuity and sexual license perfectly normal.

In an effort to prove that premarital intercourse
is a mortal sin theologians frequently adduce three
texts in which St. Paul says that those guilty of *porneia* will be excluded from the kingdom of God:
Galatians 5:19–20, Ephesians 5:5 and 1 Corinthians
6:9. In most versions *porneia* is translated as fornication. But in the first two texts it may mean adul-

tery, as it does in St. Matthew's Gospel. However, in the third text *porneia* (*pórnoi*) is distinguished from adultery (*moechoi*) and so must mean something else. While it may designate simple fornication, it is quite likely that it means prostitution and promiscuous sexual relations as it does in other Pauline texts.

The last passage customarily adduced by theologians to show that the New Testament condemns premarital sex is Acts 15:20 and 29: "I rule, then, that instead of making things more difficult for pagans who turn to God, we send them a letter telling them merely to abstain from anything polluted by idols, from fornication, from the meat of strangled animals and from blood. . . . It has been decided by the Holy Spirit and by ourselves not to saddle you with any burden beyond these essentials: you are to abstain from food sacrificed to idols, from blood, from the meat of strangled animals and from fornication. Avoid these, and you will do what is right."

A note in the Jerusalem Bible says that "this word [*porneia*] probably refers to all the irregular marriages listed in Leviticus 18." These are incestuous unions of various kinds. This same interpretation is given by Richard Dillon and Joseph Fitzmyer in the *Jerome Biblical Commentary*: "The things James forbids," they write, "seem to be four of the things proscribed by Lev. 17–18 for the alien residing in Israel: meat offered to idols (Lev. 17: 8–9), the eating of blood (Lev. 17: 10–12), the eating of strangled animals (Lev. 17:15; cf. Exod. 22:31) and intercourse with close kin (Lev. 18:6–18) . . . against this background *porneia* would refer to sexual union within certain degrees of kinship."

A fair conclusion from a study of the Old and New Testaments is this: while the bible condemns adultery, incest, prostitution and sexual licentiousness or promiscuity, it is not at all clear that it ever condemns all premarital coitus as sinful, much less premarital petting and sex play.

THE MAGISTERIUM

The Church's official magisterium has condemned premarital coitus and petting as mortal sins. However, it is significant that the magisterium did not settle the matter definitively in any of its condemnations.

Both the thirteenth ecumenical council at Lyons under Innocent IV in 1245 and the fifteenth ecumenical council at Vienne under Clement V in 1312 condemned premarital intercourse. The Council of Lyons decreed: "But concerning fornication, which an unmarried person commits with another unmarried person, there is no doubt that it is a mortal sin, since the Apostle asserts that fornicators as well as adulterers are excluded from the kingdom of God (cf. 1 Cor. 6:9)."[4] And the Council of Vienne decreed that it is a mistake to say that "kissing a woman is a mortal sin, since nature does not incline to that, but the carnal act is not a sin, since nature does incline to that, especially when one is tempted."[5]

While the sense of both of these decisions is clear enough, it is important to note that neither is a dogmatic decree. The first appears in the instruction for the Greeks, and the second is in a list of errors attributed to the Beghards and Beguines. At the end of this list the Council condemns these sects and their errors and orders that no one in the future hold, approve or defend them.[6]

On November 14, 1459, Pope Pius II condemned nine propositions attributed to an obscure canon named Zaninus of Solcia. The seventh of these errors was the opinion that debauchery outside of marriage was sinful not in itself but only because it was forbidden by ecclesiastical law.[7] Pius censured the opinions of Zaninus as "most pernicious errors."

On September 24, 1665, Pope Alexander VII rejected the opinion of the moralist Caramuel that a man who has sexual intercourse with a single woman need only confess that he committed a grave sin against chastity and not mention that this sin was intercourse.[8] The point of this decision was to maintain that coitus is a specifically distinct sin from petting and so must be clearly declared in confession. The condemnation obviously supposes that sexual intercourse with an unmarried woman is a mortal sin. The erroneous opinion of Caramuel was rejected with the censure of "at least scandalous." Another opinion of Caramuel was condemned by Pope Innocent XI in 1679 when he decreed that it was "at least scandalous and in practice dangerous" to hold that fornication is not evil in itself but only because it is forbidden by positive law.[9]

In more recent times, Pope Pius XI wrote in *Casti Cunnubii*: "Nor must we omit to remark, in fine, that since the duty entrusted to parents for the good of their children is of such high dignity and of such great importance, every use of the faculty given by God for the procreation of new life is the right and privilege of the married state alone, by the law of God and of nature, and must be confined absolutely within the sacred limits of that state."[10]

There is no ambiguity in the pope's statement: all premarital coitus is excluded. But this statement has nowhere near the solemnity of his pronouncement on artificial contraception which appears in the same encyclical letter. In comparison, his sentence concerning premarital sex appears almost as an incidental remark. It certainly does not represent a definitive magisterial decision. In fact, since it was incidental to the central doctrine that the pope was proposing in his encyclical, it is doubtful that it even qualifies as authentic non-infallible teaching.

Historically, therefore, the official Church has opposed the opinion that premarital coitus is not a grave sin. But it never condemned the opinion as heretical nor defined it as contrary to divine revelation or the Catholic faith. It is true that the Council of Lyons interpreted 1 Corinthians 6:9 as referring to simple fornication and not merely to prostitution or promiscuity; but that interpretation was given merely as a reason in support of its teaching and was not itself the object of that teaching. The most that can be proven is that on a number of occasions the Church rejected the opinion that premarital intercourse is not a grave sin but always rejected it with a rather mild censure—as a scandalous or dangerous idea.

The Church also condemned premarital petting but always with the same restraint. On March 18, 1666, Pope Alexander VII censured the following opinion of Caramuel: "There is a probable opinion which says that kissing for the carnal and sensible pleasure which arises from kissing is only a venial sin, as long as there is no danger of further consent and pollution."[11] Josef Fuchs, however, says that the exact meaning of this condemnation is not clear.[12] And Vermeersch argues that perhaps the reason for the condemnation of this opinion was its sweeping universality, since no distinctions are drawn concerning the kind or intensity of the kissing which Caramuel had in mind.[13] Whatever its meaning, the opinion is only censured by the pope as "at least scandalous."

Similarly, in 1928 P. A. Laarakkers published a book in which he asserted that incomplete sexual acts are not mortal sins; in 1929 the Holy Office ordered the book withdrawn from the market because his opinion was judged "at least dangerous in practice."

In summary, one can say that in regard to both premarital intercourse and petting there has been official vigilance over the more strict theological teaching. Contrary teaching was reproved, but always with a relatively mild censure. There certainly has been no definitive magisterial decision.

THEOLOGICAL OPINION

While there has been no historical study on premarital intimacy to match Noonan's work on contraception, theological opinion has been constant and practically unanimous, and from the beginning practicing Catholics have assumed that intercourse outside of marriage is sinful. Perhaps that is why the official magisterium has been so little concerned over the question.

It seems safe to say that for all practical purposes Catholic theologians have always and everywhere taught that premarital intercourse is a grave sin. In the seventeenth century Caramuel held that premarital intercourse was not sinful in itself but only because it was forbidden by positive law. Durandus seems to have held that it is positive legislation that makes its malice grave. In the nineteenth century Palmieri admitted sympathy with the opinion of Tamburini that while there is no doubt about the grave malice of fornication, it is very difficult to prove this by human reasoning. Theologians quarreled about the validity of each other's arguments, but no one seems to have seriously challenged the truth of the doctrine.

There has been a little more discussion on the question of premarital petting, particularly around the seventeenth century. Diaz Moreno investigated ninety moral theologians of that era and found that of these forty-seven discussed the question of whether incomplete sexual acts were grave sins. Of these, nine held that actions directed toward only slight sexual stimulation were only venial sins.[14] The most eminent of these was Thomas Sanchez. Some literature mentions that Sanchez retracted this teaching, but as Richard McCormick once pointed out, the retrac-

tion appeared in 1654 and Sanchez went to the re-
ward of all good moralists in 1610. The more lenient
opinion was resurrected in the twentieth century by
Laarakkers, Antonelli, Alberti and others until the
Holy Office ordered their books withdrawn from cir-
culation. Some discussion on this question is beginning again today, but I think it is fair to say that,
at least in regard to what has been put into print,
the stricter opinion remains practically unanimous.

THE ARGUMENTS

In support of their teaching that all premarital
coitus is a grave sin the most popular and commonly
used argument by the manualists is the argument
given by St. Thomas in II–II, 154, 3. It is put this
way by Fuchs: sexual coition is fully natural only if
it is performed by a couple who can naturally render
secure the education of a child, since the natural
end of sexual coition is the generation and education
of a child; normally the proper education of a child
can be guaranteed only within the permanent state
of marriage.[15]

The obvious difficulty with this argument is
that while it may be admitted that the proper education of a child is normally secure only within
marriage, it can also be guaranteed in other ways.

What is more, this argument does not seem to touch the cases of sexual intercourse that will certainly be sterile (e.g., with a woman who has had a hysterectomy or is past her menopause).

St. Thomas did not fail to see this difficulty and responded that laws are determined according to what commonly occurs, not according to what may occur in particular instances. Even though the bad effect that a law is designed to guard against will not in fact result, the nature of the action remains the same in every case.

Perhaps there is more in Thomas' answer than I can see. It is true that universal laws cannot take into account an infinite number of singular possibilities and therefore have to be framed or formulated in general terms or, as St. Thomas says, according to what normally occurs. But it would seem that the laws then apply in the concrete only to those normal or usual situations where the evil that the law guards against de facto exists, and that the law is irrelevant and does not apply to those situations in which the evil to be avoided is certainly absent. It is true that the nature of the act does not change in these latter situations, but the act is not evil in its physical structure but only because of its evil consequences. If the evil consequence certainly does not and will not result, why is the act in that case to be judged evil? To argue in this way is not to fall into any kind of extreme situationism or consequentialism in ethical thinking. It is only to say that if a certain act is forbidden only because of a specific evil that will frequently result, there is no reason to say that it is still forbidden in those instances where the evil will certainly not result.

All that can be concluded is that the Thomistic argument has a force that is relevant to many if not most situations. The danger of premarital pregnancy with all its economic and social consequences for the child, the young couple and their families is still a problem in our contemporary society. To argue that illegitimate pregnancies are no longer a problem in "the post-pill paradise" is a bit too simple. Not only does it too easily solve the moral question about the practice of contraception both within and outside of marriage, it also overlooks the sociological data about illegitimate pregnancies even in our contraceptive age. Contraceptive means of every sort—pills, condoms, vaginal foams, douches, diaphragms, rhythm —are familiar and available to most young people today. But there are other related factors such as carelessness, suddenness of emotion and spontaneity, as well as some girls' conscious or unconscious desire to become pregnant. Therefore it is not too much of a surprise that Vance Packard's recent survey of college students reveals that while the fear of pregnancy has declined among young people the incidence of it has not.

Most current theological literature takes a different tack. The arguments against premarital intercourse are more personalistic. As Rollo May pointed out, men do not only fuck or screw, they also make love. And *making love* is not just a euphemism for *fucking;* it is a quite different human experience. Sexual intercourse is a natural sign of total, unreserved self-giving. At the moment of orgasm the individual's personality is lost in an interpenetration of the other self. As modern metaphysical anthropology tells us, corporeity is intersubjectivity. That is to say, I am my body; I am my sexuality. Coition is not just genital commingling with one endocrine system calling out to another. Coition is expressive of the person, and to be authentic and not a lie it must correspond to the existing relationship of the person. From this analysis of the meaning of human sexuality, it follows that its authentic actuation demands that it be expressive of a love that is total self-donation, that is to say, a final, permanent and exclusive commitment. If it is less, it is a lie, a betrayal of the genuine meaning of the sign and a trivialization of the genuine meaning of human sexuality. But if it is not less, then it is what we mean when we say "marriage."

Paul Ramsey accepts this argument but makes one distinction. He says that where engaged couples are concerned we must distinguish between premarital and preceremonial. He argues that "if a couple mean to express the fact that their lives are united and that they are now willing to accept all that is entailed in sexual intercourse as their unity in one flesh," then they are in the moral sense already married, and their coition may be preceremonial but is not premarital.[16]

Richard McCormick, however, thinks that Ramsey's view is too narrow. McCormick argues that the term *premarital* must be understood in relation to the total reality of marriage and the total reality of the persons. "Marriage," he says, "as totally understood is an ecclesial and social reality. The person is an ecclesial and social being. Hence, intercourse performed with what the parties call 'marriage consent' is premarital . . . if this consent is not socially or ecclesially valid. After all, one's ability to effect something by consent is conditioned by his ecclesial reality."[17]

From the point of view of Catholic ecclesiology, what McCormick has in mind is that the Church vindicates to herself competence over the sacramental marriage of baptized persons in such a way that she can establish even diriment or invalidating impediments, as she does for instance when she requires the observance of the canonical form. But it is important to notice the new turn that the argument has taken. The reason why intercourse between engaged couples is wrong in certain instances is rooted in positive law. But positive law, even that which establishes diriment impediments, does not bind in every case. Catholic moralists and canonists have not only admitted the validity of clandestine marriages before the existence of the diriment impediment; they have admitted that the law ceases to bind under certain grave difficulties, for instance, when a ceremony before a priest and two witnesses could not be arranged.

In other words, when there is a proportionately grave inconvenience, preceremonial intercourse is not premarital intercourse, even if we take into consideration one's ecclesial reality. "No preceremonial intercourse," therefore, is not an absolute principle and never was considered one by Catholic moralists. Exceptions are possible when there is serious inconvenience, and it would be a useful exercise in theological casuistry to explore the kinds of reasons that today might justify a young couple's situational departure from the general norm. In general, however, the new personalistic approach is persuasive. Bertocci's presentation and development of it is as good as I have seen.[18] But that is not to say that it is without its difficulties or needs no further clarifications.

In the matter of premarital petting the fundamental principle that has guided theological casuistry is this: any directly voluntary sexual or venereal reaction, no matter how slight, is grave matter. This does not, of course, imply that theologians therefore judged that all petting was grave matter. A skillful application of the principle of double effect allowed them to steer a more realistic path in the real world. But the principle itself is a strange one. The reasoning behind it is this: the complete sexual act outside of marriage is gravely deordinate; but the incomplete act is designed of its very nature to form one organic whole with the complete act; therefore the incomplete act is also gravely deordinate.[19]

This argument is by no means convincing, but one does hear some rather stupid objections to it. One objection commonly heard is that theologians admit parvity of matter in every area except sex. The implication, presumably, is that moral theologians are so hung up on sex that they handle it with arbitrary rigidity. The truth is that the principle they apply here is applied to all areas where any degree contains the substantial violation (e.g., perjury, blasphemy, hatred of God, simony) or where the matter is indivisible (e.g., homicide, adultery).

The problem is not with the principle concerning parvity of matter. The problem is that it is not clear that this principle is correctly applied to sexual activity. It rightly applies here only if incomplete sexual actuation tends, as the argument claims it does, of its nature to the perfect act, so that of its nature it is an organic part of an indivisible organic whole. But whether all, even the most insignificant and transient, sexual activity tends of its very nature to orgasm can certainly be questioned.

3. Masturbation

No OTHER form of sexual activity has been more frequently discussed, more roundly condemned and more universally practiced than masturbation.[1] Even infrahuman animals have been caught in the act. Zoologists inform us that masturbation, sometimes to the point of orgasm, has been observed among the male and occasionally the female members of the following species: the rat, chinchilla, rabbit, porcupine, squirrel, horse, cow, elephant, dog, baboon, monkey and chimpanzee. According to Kinsey, 95% of American men and 70% of American women have masturbated.[2] The estimates for adolescent boys vary between 60% and 100%. The most recurrent figure seems to be about 85%. Unfortunately, these figures provide no indication whether the masturbation reported is habitual, frequent, occasional or seldom.

Apparently two-month-old babies sometimes manipulate their genitals. Among three-year-olds the practice is more common and sometimes is accompanied by an erection, although this activity is not specifically a sexual one. Masturbators of six or seven have more pronounced sensual feelings, without of course experiencing orgasm. At the age of puberty masturbation with orgasm is possible and is initiated by a large number of children. This practice sometimes continues after marriage and is especially likely during the temporary absence or after the death of the spouse.

The ordinary method of masturbating among males is to grip the penis in the hand and move the hand back and forth along the penile shaft at the suitable pressure and speed. Orgasm is generally reached within two to three minutes, sometimes within thirty seconds. If there is a desire to prolong the pleasurable experience orgasm is sometimes delayed for as long as thirty minutes. For women the ordinary technique is to stimulate the clitoris by rubbing the vulva with the hand or fingers. According to the studies of Masters and Johnson, the most effective way is by friction on the side of the clitoris rather than directly on it.[3]

There are also other less usual methods. Some

men, for instance, rub their penis against an object, such as the bed. Some even engage in self-fellation, although for most men this is an anatomical impossibility. Self-fellation is a common means of masturbation among some monkeys, chimpanzees and other primates. Kinsey remarks that in his psychic drive the human animal occasionally seems to be more mammalian than his anatomy allows him to be. Women sometimes use dildoes or rub their thighs together in a rhythmical way. McCary reports that in the nineteenth century French doctors were particularly worried about an occupational hazard of seamstresses: as they treadled their sewing machines the up and down movements of their legs sometimes caused orgasms, and in at least one establishment a matron was appointed to circulate among the seamstresses to watch for runaway machines.[4]

In the past medical men have attributed countless physical and mental disorders to masturbation. Today there are many psychiatrists and psychologists who consider masturbation desirable and presume that anyone who does not masturbate is abnormal. From the evidence we have, the truth seems to be that in itself masturbation is not harmful either physically or psychologically. Sometimes one hears that while occasional masturbation is harmless, excessive masturbation is not. But it is not easy to understand what is meant by excessive masturbation. The average adolescent is easily capable of three or four ejaculations per week, and some are capable of seven to fourteen. When one reaches the limit of his physiological endurance, the organism is no longer responsive to the erotic stimuli until it is adequately rested.

Although masturbation in itself appears to be harmless both physically and psychologically, to speak of masturbation in itself is not sufficient. Masturbation, like most things, can be judged and evaluated only in its existential context, and the existential context in which it occurs is a religious, social, cultural and personal one. In some personalities, especially introverted and conscientious ones, masturbation often results in such psychic disturbances as worry, conscious or unconscious guilt and anxiety. Half of the female masturbators sampled by Kinsey suffered some such psychic disturbances. It is not surprising that many people are considerably disturbed when they masturbate, since masturbation has been condemned as sinful in our Judaeo-Christian culture. Freud and many psychoanalysts have contributed to the source of worry and anxiety, since they classify masturbation as infantile, immature and a personality defect which often deserves psychiatric attention when practiced by an adult. Masturbation also causes some people to worry about being sex-

results in, or is consequence of ? (see next page)

ually inept with the opposite sex or about not being in control of their own behavior. Since it is not an adequate heterosexual experience, one that is psychically as well as physically satisfying, masturbation often leaves the masturbator with a feeling of inadequacy, inferiority, diffidence and depression. What is more, the causality here appears to be reciprocal since masturbation is sometimes the result or symptom of a psychic disturbance.

A number of psychologists today conclude that there would be no problem with masturbation if it were not for the misinformation, myths and religious taboos that surround it. They advise us to educate young people to an understanding that there is nothing wrong with masturbation and so relieve them of unnecessary fears and feelings of guilt. This argument, however, proceeds too quickly. It rests on the assumption that masturbation is in fact morally good or indifferent. Empirical science has no way to verify this assumption. It is true that masturbation is statistically normal, but it does not necessarily follow that it is therefore ethically normal and morally neutral. Scripture tells us that all men are liars (Ps. 116:11), but it does not follow that lying is morally neutral. It is also true that masturbation does not cause physical or mental illness, but that does not tell us much about its human significance, its human meaning. Physical and mental health are not the only values in life. A Christian moral evaluation of masturbation remains to be made, and it must be made according to its own norms and principles.

SACRED SCRIPTURE

The Old Testament contains no moral prohibition of masturbation. We read in Leviticus 15:16, "When a man has a seminal discharge, he must wash his whole body with water and shall be unclean until evening," and in Deuteronomy 23:9–11, "If any man among you is unclean by reason of a nocturnal emission, he must go out of the camp and not come into it again; toward evening he must wash himself, and he may return to the camp at sunset." But the reasons underlying this legislation are hygienic and cultic rather than moral.

In the New Testament there are three passages that are usually urged against masturbation: 1 Thessalonians 4:3–4; Romans 1:24; and 1 Corinthians 6:10.

1 Thessalonians 4:3–4 reads: "What God wants is for you all to be holy. He wants you to keep away from fornication, and each of you to know how to use the body that belongs to him in a way that is holy and honorable, not giving way to selfish lust like the pagans who do not know God." Exegetes are divided

on the correct translation of this text. *Tò scheûos* literally means "vessel" and is often used to designate the body which is, as it were, the vessel or instrument of the soul. But it can also be used to designate one's wife, as it is in 1 Peter 3:7. If it means wife here, as it may, then there is no question of masturbation. But if it is correctly translated here as meaning one's own body, as is more likely the case, one still cannot conclude that a condemnation of masturbation is necessarily implied. What is condemned is using one's body in an unholy and dishonorable way, giving in to selfish lust like the pagans who do not know God. What Paul had in mind was the sexual licentiousness and promiscuity that was considered perfectly normal in the pagan society of his time. That a specific condemnation of masturbation is also implied is certainly possible, but there is no way that one can be sure. One can read such a specific condemnation into the text if he already assumes that masturbation is an unholy and dishonorable use of the body. But if one is looking for proof, he does not find it here.

In Romans 1:24, describing God's anger against the pagans, Paul writes: "That is why God left them to their filthy enjoyments and the practices with which they dishonor their own bodies." There is nothing conclusive in this text against masturbation since it is most likely from the context that Paul is referring specifically to the sin of sodomy.

In 1 Corinthians 6:10, however, Paul condemns the *manakoì* who are expressly distinguished from sodomites (*arsenokoîtai*). *Manakoì* literally means the soft or effeminate, and in this context it most likely signifies not masturbators but catamites, i.e., small boys kept for the purpose of pederasty.

Other New Testament texts are sometimes adduced, but they are even less successful in demonstrating the immorality of masturbation.

THE MAGISTERIUM

Condemnations of masturbation by the Church's official magisterium have been plentiful. The first official teaching against it appears to be in a letter of Pope Leo IX, *Ad Splendidum Mentis,* sent to St. Peter Damian in 1054, in which the pope said that masturbators should not be admitted to sacred orders.[5] This same official policy continues in our day. An instruction from the Sacred Congregation of Religious, dated February 2, 1961, says: ". . . any candidate who has a habit of solitary sins and who has not given well-founded hope that he can break this habit within a period of time to be determined prudently, is not to be admitted to the novitiate. . . . A much stricter policy must be followed in admission to perpetual profession and advancement to Sacred Orders. No one should be admitted to perpetual

vows or promoted to Sacred Orders unless he has
acquired a firm habit of continency and has given in
every case consistent proof of habitual chastity over
a period of at least one year. If within this year . . .
doubt should arise because of new falls, the candidate is to be barred from . . . Sacred Orders."[6]

In 1666 Alexander VII condemned as at least
scandalous the opinion that masturbation, sodomy
and bestiality are sins of the same specific malice and
therefore it is sufficient to confess that one procured
pollution.[7] And in 1679 Pope Innocent XI condemned as at least scandalous and dangerous in practice the opinion of Caramuel that "masturbation is
not forbidden by the law of nature; therefore if God
had not forbidden it, it would be good and sometimes gravely obligatory."[8]

On September 2, 1904, the Sacred Penitentiary
declared that the complete masturbatory acts of a
woman during the absence of her husband are gravely
illicit and that any confessor who approves this practice should be denounced to the Holy See.[9] And on
August 2, 1929, the Holy Office was asked: "Whether
direct masturbation is permitted for the purpose of
obtaining semen for the scientific detection of the
contagious disease 'blenorragia' and its cure." The
answer was: "In the negative."[10] The reply was ap-
proved by Pope Pius XI and ordered published.[11]

In more recent times Pope Pius XII said in his
address on the education of the Christian conscience:

With the selfsame authority we declare to educators and to young people also: the divine commandment of purity of soul and body still holds without any diminution for the youth of today. They have also the moral obligation and, with the help of grace, the possibility of preserving themselves pure. We reject, therefore, as erroneous the affirmation of those who regard lapses as inevitable in the adolescent years, and therefore as not worthy of being taken into consideration, as if they were not grave faults, because, they add, as a general rule passion destroys the liberty requisite if an act is to be morally imputable.[12]

This statement of Pius XII has as its substantive content the assertion that the divine commandment of purity still holds without any diminution for the youth of today. Although it does not say anything specifically about masturbation, one can hardly doubt that the pope had this in mind. The statement was made at the time of the famous "Oraison affair" and can best be understood in that context. In 1952 Marc Oraison, a physician, psychiatrist and priest, published his doctoral dissertation *Vie chrétienne et problèmes de la sexualité*. Ford and Kelly summarize his conclusion:

Almost all mankind is so sexually immature, and so much dominated consciously or unconsciously by passion, that in practice and as a general rule we must presume that sexual sins are only materially grave, that is, the person who commits them is not subjectively guilty of mortal sin. Sins of masturbation, homosexuality, fornication and adultery, and conjugal onanism must be presumed in the vast majority of cases to be only material mortal sins. Those who confess them should be properly instructed as to their grave malice, and gradually educated to that (rare) stage of sexual maturity where they will no longer occur. But while they continue to occur, the sacraments are not to be refused, and the victims of this pathology should be instructed that it is permissible to receive Holy Communion after these things happen without first confessing them.[13]

Oraison's book was placed nominatim on the Index early in 1953, and this fact was published in January, 1955. Oraison immediately submitted to the decision of the Holy Office and withdrew his opinion.

The whole matter is still extremely delicate. As recently as July 15, 1961, the following Monitum was issued by the Holy Office:

Since many dangerous opinions are being published and spread regarding the sins incurred by violations of the Sixth Commandment and regarding the imputability of human actions, the Sacred Congregation of the Holy Office establishes the following norms for public knowledge: Bishops, presidents of faculties of theology, rectors of seminaries and schools for Religious must require that those whose duty it is to teach moral theology and similar disciplines comply exactly with the traditional teaching of the Church. Ecclesiastical censors must use great caution in censoring and passing judgment on books and publications which deal with the sixth precept of the Decalogue.[14]

THEOLOGICAL OPINION

Although there is no historical study of the theological opinion on masturbation that is comparable to Noonan's study on contraception, it can be safely said that the theological opinion asserting that all directly willed pollution is gravely illicit is ancient and practically unanimous. Clear and explicit statements begin to appear around the sixth century. Although St. Alphonsus cites eleven authors who hold that masturbation admits of parvity of matter, from about the tenth century the stricter opinion became express and practically unanimous.

The theological arguments, however, have been less than satisfactory. One argument was based on the frustration of the human seed that occurs in masturbation. But the fact is that it has been relatively rare in the history of human seed that it has not been frustrated. Most human seed has been and always will be wasted. It is without issue not only in nocturnal pollutions and in the copula of the sterile (e.g., with women after menopause or with fertile women during most of the month) but also in fertile intercourse where one sperm is successful and hundreds of thousands perish. Besides, this argument does not explain why female masturbation is judged equally wrong.

Another argument has been that if masturbation was not gravely forbidden, the good of the species would suffer, since many people would not marry. Aside from the questionable assumption that many people would find masturbation an adequate substitute for heterosexual intercourse, this argument does not conclude to any intrinsic malice in masturbation. It is not surprising, therefore, that both of these arguments have been abandoned.

The contemporary argument against masturbation is expressed succinctly by Josef Fuchs: Union with a partner of the opposite sex is required for sexual actuation in order that the mode of actuation might be of itself generative and at the same time an intimate expression of love. A solitary act would be a perversion of the act which of its nature is social not individual.[15]

In 1968 Richard McCormick explicated this analysis:

> My own tentative analysis would build as follows. (1) The objective meaning of sexual acts is to be an expression of a special kind of love rela-

tionship (totally self-giving and procreative in character). Sex acts get *human* meaning from being expressions of such a relationship. (2) Sexual acts which do not express this relationship are withdrawals from the values and foods of this relationship, hence the use of sex without *human* meaning, hence the misuse of a symbol. Thus the basic malice of any deordinate sex act is its failure to be an expression of this special relation, to be human. (3) All deordinate sex acts represent this removal from relationship and its values. Their specificity consists in their degree of withdrawal from and rejection of this relationship and the values embedded in it. (4) The values of this special relationship (the stable, personal, loving union of man and woman and the perfection this leads to; generous and responsible fecundity) are built upon and reflect the more basic lines of the meaning of our sexuality: *intersubjectivity and heterosexuality*. Hence all deordinate sexual acts are variously a rejection of, a refusal to grow in our own intersubjectivity and heterosexuality. And since I am my body, my sexuality, deordinate acts are acts of the person *in rejection of his own growth*. (5) The malice of masturbation, then, is as follows: (a) *Generically,* it is, with all deordinate sex acts, a withdrawal from the relationship whose goods give human meaning to sex expression; and therefore, with all sex acts, it represents a rejection of one's intersubjectivity and heterosexuality; (b) *Specifically,* masturbation is a rather total withdrawal from this relationship, and is a rather *total* rejection of one's radical intersubjectivity and heterosexuality. (Parenthetically, such a rejection is obviously harmful to an individual. And thus ironically, self-petting, self-caressing shows up ultimately as self-hating.)[16]

McCormick points out that contemporary literature increasingly finds the significance of masturbation in an understanding of sexuality similar to the one he presented. For instance, in *Love and Marriage* Gibert writes: "In order to correctly gauge the significance of this elementary sexual act of masturbation, one must use as a point of reference the real and true notion of human sexuality, which cannot be conceived outside the mutual love and faithfulness of a man and woman intimately joined in the unity of body, mind and emotions, and performing a creative act that involves the total gift of one's self to the other. The act of masturbation is not just a single but a double shifting of the sexual act away from its purposeful end, first because it presupposes the absence of all emotional contact and responsible pledge, and secondly because it utterly nullifies the procreative intent of human love."[17]

In a talk to the Catholic Theological Society of America in 1966 Charles Curran argued for a re-evaluation of traditional teaching on the gravity of matter in masturbation.[18] He merely initiated what he called an "exploratory discussion" among profes-

sional theologians. He argued that a single masturbatory act does not create a presumption for a
fundamental option and therefore is not grave matter. Most of his arguments against the traditional
teaching were directed against theological analyses
which are already outdated and abandoned, but one
of the questions he raised can be directed against the
contemporary analyses of Fuchs and McCormick as
well. "It does not seem," he said, "that a single masturbatory action can constitute a substantial inversion of an order of very great importance. Perhaps in
the past theologians have illegitimately transferred
to the individual act the importance that belongs to
the sexual faculty. I am not saying that individual
actions are never important; but in the total consideration of masturbation, individual actions do not
always constitute a substantial inversion of human
sexuality."[19]

This, however, is precisely the conclusion that
the analyses of Fuchs and McCormick try to come to,
namely that an individual masturbatory action is a
substantial inversion of human sexuality. The question now under consideration has nothing to do with
subjective imputability but rather with objective
morality. There are, of course, a host of reasons why
the objectively immoral may not be subjectively imputable, and we will discuss that question below.
The point at issue now is the objective morality of

masturbation, and the question is whether a single act is grave matter.

It seems to me that the analyses of Fuchs and McCormick rightly conclude only to the serious immorality of habitual masturbation over a long period of time. To stunt one's growth intersubjectively and heterosexually is a serious matter. To pervert the natural human meaning of sexuality in a substantive way would appear to be a grave deordination. But it is not clear how a single act of masturbation or a short series of these acts is a substantial inversion of growth or a substantive withdrawal from the human meaning of sexuality as unitive and procreative.

If someone were to ask, When does this prolonged series become grave matter? I would have to answer that the application of the general principle to individuals, whether young, old, single or married, would be so diverse that any further casuistry beyond the principle would be practically useless. All that can be said is that masturbation is objectively immoral to the extent that it in fact impedes intersubjective and heterosexual growth and to the extent that it is an inversion of the human meaning of sexuality. If it does this in a substantial way, it is grave matter; if it does it in a slight way, it is light matter. An individual would presumably be formally culpable of grave sin only if he deliberately chose or did not seriously endeavor to break the kind of habit which would qualify, in accord with our principle, as gravely deordinate for him.

Perhaps it can be legitimately argued against my analysis and in defense of the analyses of Fuchs and McCormick that (1) a single act of masturbation is a substantial inversion of heterosexual and interpersonal growth objectively speaking, since objectively speaking it is in itself narcissistic (even though the subjective affect of narcissism might be missing), and that (2) a single act is a substantial perversion of the objective meaning of human sexuality, since it is in itself a negation of its total significance and finality, interpersonal union and procreation. These, in fact, are the assertions of Fuchs and McCormick, but convincing proof is missing. At the very least, the whole question of the objective immorality of masturbation deserves more study, reflection and discussion among theologians.

PRACTICAL CONCLUSIONS

When they spoke of pastoral practice the moralists of the past always adjusted or tempered the hard line they took when discussing the objective morality of masturbation in the abstract. They conceded that subjective culpability was often diminished or removed by such factors as ignorance, overpowering passion, inveterate habit and compulsive urges. This was the same tack taken by Marc Oraison: he admitted the objectively grave malice of masturbation but found excuse in subjective conditions. It seems fair to say that he did go too far in this approach, however, since underlying his practical conclusions was the assumption that the vast majority of men are the victims of sexual pathology.

If Marc Oraison went too far in minimizing subjective responsibility, the older authors did not go far enough. They went as far as their knowledge of the human act would allow them. What was lacking to them and is available to us is a better theological understanding of the nature of mortal sin. When talking about the difference between mortal and venial sin one must inevitably face the question that bothered St. Augustine: if every sin is a violation of God's will, why is not every sin against the love of God and therefore grave? The nominalists and Baius answered that the difference is simply due to the decree of God who freely decides that some sins are mortal and some venial. Unsatisfied with such an extrinsic explanation, many theologians argued that the difference is real and rooted in the matter of the sins: grave sins are substantially opposed to the order willed by God whereas venial sins are not.

A growing number of theologians today, among them Josef Fuchs and Piet Schoonenberg, are not entirely satisfied with this explanation.[20] They prefer to say that the gravity of a sin does not depend primarily on the gravity of the matter but rather on a man's disposition of himself in relation to God, his last end. A sin is therefore grave or mortal if the opposition to God that is present in every sin is penetrated by a man in the deepest center of his person, so that he freely and consciously, though not reflexly, denies love to God above all things else.

According to this explanation, a man's relation to God is determined by his fundamental option, for it is by his fundamental option that he totally disposes of himself either for or against his last end. The fundamental option normally is not present explicitly or in the reflex consciousness. It is implicitly involved in a moral act concerning some particular object and it takes place consciously and freely but in a way that is not reflex or thematic.

Therefore it is possible to commit a mortal sin in slight matter, not only because of an erroneous conscience but because in the sinful act a man so penetrates its evil and opposition to God that he determines his fundamental option away from God as his ultimate end. It is also possible to commit a venial sin in grave matter, again not only because of an erroneous conscience but because of a lack of personal penetration of the act. Even though one has conceptual knowledge and advertence to the material malice of an act plus the free consent of the will with reflex consciousness, he may not have a sufficiently deep and intense perception of the moral value involved or, at least implicitly and non-reflexly, of the relation of this act to his last end.

The most that can be said about the matter of the act is that it establishes a presumption: if the matter is grave the sin is ordinarily mortal; if the matter is light the sin is ordinarily venial.[21] A man cannot normally perceive in the depths of his soul the relation of his person to his ultimate end in an act that is concerned with light matter. Hence this act will not normally be a true total disposition of himself in relation to God. Ordinarily a man has evaluative knowledge and an implicit and non-reflex apprehension of the relation of a grave act to his last end. This act ordinarily will represent a determination of his fundamental option.

If we apply this conception of mortal sin to masturbation, I think that it is fair to say that it is very unlikely that anyone changes his fundamental option two or three times a week. One can presume that the average adolescent who has a fairly deep-rooted habit of masturbation is not guilty of mortal sin in every act. Each case, of course, must be judged in its own circumstances, but I think that this presumption is valid and can be acted upon in almost all cases. This does not mean that there is no culpability and no sin, only that it is not mortal. The adolescent should be told this plainly. It should be explained to him that every act is not a mortal sin for him because of his habit and that he may receive the Eucharist without confessing it. He should be told that although his acts of masturbation are not mortally sinful, they are a serious challenge to his growth and so demand in response a serious effort on his part to rid himself of them. It is here that he will in all likelihood be faced with the occasion of making a genuine fundamental option: a serious determination to grow out of the habit will indicate one fundamental option; a decision to make no serious effort to break it will indicate another.

Although confession is not necessary before receiving the Eucharist, frequent confession or talks with a priest outside of confession will often be useful to help overcome the habit, to avoid discouragement and to understand and get at any underlying problem of which masturbation is only a symptom.

In cases other than the habitual adolescent masturbator, such as the occasional masturbator or the married man who masturbates, a less generalized judgment will have to be made. The factors influencing this behavior will be varied and often complex. A prudent judgment will have to be made in the light of the same principles and in accord with the particular circumstances of the situation.

4. Celibacy

It is hardly giving away secrets to say that there is a debate going on in the Church over the question of clerical celibacy. What might come as a surprise to some is the breadth of that debate. In fact, there sometimes appear to be two separate debates going on side by side with no attempt to integrate them.

One debate is taking place in the theological literature. It is being conducted by professional theologians from their point of view and with their sources of knowledge. In this debate it appears that the opinion favoring mandatory celibacy is winning. The other debate is going on among the ordinary clergy and laity. It is being conducted in the mass media of television and the news magazines, in formal colloquia and in the informal talk of living rooms and cocktail parties. In this debate the argument runs mainly along pragmatic lines and it seems that the opinion favoring optional celibacy is winning.

In addition to the theological and the popular arguments there is also what might be called the political argument, such as that going on between the Dutch Pastoral Council and the Holy See. It is the outcome of this sort of argument that will be decisive. Whether and to what extent the Holy See will relax the present legislation on clerical celibacy cannot be predicted with certainty, but for what it is worth I will make a prediction before I have finished.

In the meantime, it will be useful to try to understand all the values that are at stake. To do so it will be necessary to integrate the theological considerations with the practical ones. It is obviously not enough to debate the matter of clerical celibacy on merely pragmatic grounds, as if sacred virginity were not fundamentally a Christian mystery, and as if theology and revelation had nothing to say. Nor, on the other hand, is it possible to defend from an aprioristic stance the legislation of ideals, no matter how noble, without considering how such legislation will in fact affect men's lives.

There is one thing more that should be noted.

Although the popular or journalistic argument is often clouded by caricature, shortsightedness and muddled thinking, it cannot be presumed that the theological argument is necessarily more important or closer to the truth. When the theologians in the Eastern Church were confused about the divinity of Christ and debating with subtle arguments whether Mary was the mother of God, the ordinary clergy and laity, who were fairly innocent of theology, were marching and rioting in the streets, hollering with united voice, "Theotokos." While Thomas Aquinas and other great medieval minds could not see how Mary could possibly be immaculately conceived, the people, calmly ignoring the theologians, kept praying to Mary Conceived Without Sin and celebrating her feast on December 8. God's Holy Spirit does not blow only into the ears of theologians. He blows where he wills.

One place where the Holy Spirit has left his mark is Sacred Scripture, and it is there that we will first turn our attention.

SACRED SCRIPTURE

In the Old Testament a cultic purity consisting in temporary abstinence from sexual relations was prescribed before exercising sacred duties (Exod.

19:15) or before eating consecrated bread reserved for the priests (1 Sam. 21:4). Virginity was highly esteemed in a bride (Exod. 22:15; Deut. 22:13–21), but was never valued as something to be permanently maintained.

Christian esteem for permanent virginity as an ascetic ideal draws its inspiration mainly from the example of Jesus and Mary. But there are two texts from the New Testament that are adduced in support of this stance. The first is from St. Matthew's Gospel, 19:10–12: "The disciples said to him, 'If that is how things are between husband and wife, it is not advisable to marry.' But he replied, 'It is not everyone who can accept what I have said, but only those to whom it is granted. There are eunuchs born that way from their mother's womb, there are eunuchs made so by men and there are eunuchs who have made themselves that way for the sake of the kingdom of heaven. Let anyone accept this who can.' "

Although Sixtus, Origen and certain Egyptian monks took this talk about eunuchs in an excessively physical sense, the common interpretation of this passage is that given by John McKenzie in the *Jerome Biblical Commentary*: ". . . it is possible for one to renounce marriage because of the reign of God." The invitation of Jesus, "Let anyone accept this who can," was a daring and revolutionary thought in a Jewish context. Before Jesus the ideal of permanent celibacy for any reason simply did not exist.

The note in the Jerusalem Bible confirms this exegesis but expresses it badly. It says, "Christ invites to perpetual continence those who would consecrate themselves entirely to the kingdom of God." It is an outmoded idea, of course, to think that all Christians, married and celibate, are not invited to "consecrate themselves entirely to the kingdom of God." As Schillebeeckx points out, a comparison of the working draft with the final text of *Lumen Gentium* shows that Vatican II rejected this notion.[1] The Council teaches that all Christians, without exception, are called to total dedication to the kingdom; celibacy only gives a certain facility, makes it easier.[2]

This common exegesis, however, is not the only one. Jacques Dupont and Quentin Quesnell find serious difficulty in reading Matthew 19:12 as a call to consecrated celibacy.[3] Resurrecting an ancient interpretation of Clement of Alexandria, they read it rather as referring to the preceding verses, 2–9, which conclude with these words of Jesus about divorce: ". . . the man who divorces his wife—I am not speaking of fornication—and marries another, is guilty of adultery." According to Dupont and Quesnell the eunuchs for the kingdom in Matthew 19:12

are those married men in Matthew 19:9 who separate from their wives because of adultery and, as long as the woman lives, are unable to marry again. This exegesis assumes as true what is only one possible and highly debatable interpretation of Matthew 19:9. But with this assumption, the same teaching about the indissolubility of marriage runs from verses 1 through 19. Jesus teaches that divorce and remarriage is tantamount to adultery. The apostles object to this hard teaching by saying that then it is better not to marry in the first place. Jesus, rather than accepting their objection, insists on his teaching and says that it is a mystery that the world cannot grasp but which stands as a challenge to faith and can only be accomplished for the sake of the kingdom.

This is a possible interpretation and so I note it. But it is one that probably will not receive much attention from exegetes. In the first place, exegetes today are not so ready to accept the interpretation of Matthew 19:9 as rejecting all divorce, even on account of adultery. Secondly and more importantly, they usually do not see the saying of Jesus in verses 2–9 as the historical context of his saying in verses 10–12. Rather, they generally locate the two sayings as separate historical events.

The other New Testament passage dealing with celibacy is 1 Corinthians 7:25–35:

About remaining celibate, I have no directions from the Lord but give my own opinion as one who, by the Lord's mercy, has stayed faithful. Well then, I believe that in these present times of stress this is right: that it is good for a man to stay as he is. If you are tied to a wife, do not look for freedom; if you are free of a wife, then do not look for one. But if you marry, it is no sin, and it is not a sin for a young girl to get married. They will have their troubles, though, in their married life, and I should like to spare you that.

Brothers, this is what I mean: our time is growing short. Those who have wives should live as though they had none, and those who mourn should live as though they had nothing to mourn for; those who are enjoying life should live as though there were nothing to laugh about; those whose life is buying things should live as though they had nothing of their own; and those who have to deal with the world should not become engrossed in it. I say this because the world as we know it is passing away.

I would like to see you free from all worry. An unmarried man can devote himself to the Lord's affairs, all he need worry about is pleasing the Lord; but a married man has to bother about the world's affairs and devote himself to pleasing his wife; he is torn two ways. In the same way an unmarried woman, like a young girl, can devote herself to the Lord's affairs; all she need worry about is being holy in body and spirit. The married woman, on the other hand, has to worry about the world's affairs and devote herself to pleasing her husband. I say this only to help you, not to put a halter around your necks, but simply to make sure that everything is as it should be, and that you give your undivided attention to the Lord.

No long exegesis of this passage is needed. In the *Jerome Biblical Commentary* Richard Kugelman calls attention to the eschatological framework of Paul's teaching here. For Paul the eschaton became a present reality with the resurrection of Jesus and is now advancing to its final stage. By faith and hope the baptized Christian already lives in the future, awaiting the second coming of the Lord. Paul counsels virginity over marriage during this period of expectation, because it is easier for the virgin to be detached from the things of this world which is passing away and so easier for him to devote himself singlemindedly to the Lord.

In neither of these New Testament texts is any connection made between celibacy and priesthood. The connection of celibacy is with baptism not orders. In the Pastoral Epistles Paul does not make celibacy a requirement for either priesthood or diaconate. It remains a counsel for the clergy as for all Christians. However, he does make his other counsel—that a widower not remarry—a strict requirement for both priests and deacons (cf. 1 Tim. 3:2 and 12; Titus 1:6).

SACERDOTALIS COELIBATUS

Celibacy became joined to sacred orders in the course of Christian history. In the Eastern Church the Council of Nicaea (325) forbade marriage after the reception of higher orders "according to an ancient tradition of the Church." The Synod of Trullo (692), confirming the prevailing custom, enacted the following legislation: bishops were obliged to live in continence if they were married before ordination; priests, deacons and subdeacons were not allowed to marry after ordination, but if they were married before they were allowed to stay with their wives and continue normal sexual relations. In principle these regulations of Trullo still apply in the Eastern Church. Although marriage after ordination has been tolerated for subdeacons and occasionally even for deacons and priests since the seventeenth century, in principle the present law in the Eastern Church is similar to that in the West in that it forbids all marriage *after* ordination.

In the Western Church the Synod of Elvira (305) made celibacy obligatory for the higher clergy. Particular legislation multiplied until at the Second Lateran Council (1139) a diriment impediment was established: marriages of subdeacons, deacons and priests were not only illicit but also invalid if contracted after ordination. This is the legislation that was confirmed at Trent and found its way into the *Codex Iuris Canonici*. On June 23, 1967, Pope Paul VI announced in his encyclical letter *Sacerdotalis Coelibatus* that this legislation will remain the same. He confirmed this decision in his public reaction to the recommendations of the Dutch Pastoral Council.

From our present vantage point I think that it is clear that Pope Paul's encyclical was issued prematurely. The argument was not yet finished and should have been left to run its course. The forces in the Church were such that the encyclical could not have cut off the debate. Today the argument is still running at near intensity pitch. I do not see anything disrespectful in this, if only because Church discipline is always open to reexamination. However, any responsible discussion of the question after June 23, 1967, cannot be conducted independent of or without a thorough knowledge of this important document.

The pope begins by reviewing the principal objections that are being raised against the present discipline. He lists seven: (1) In the New Testament celibacy is optional not mandatory, and the New Testament should be our model today. (2) The ancient Church which tied celibacy to office had an overly pessimistic view of sex and so considered celibacy a kind of cultic purity for priests. (3) Some men may have a call to ministry without having a call to celibacy, since these are distinct charisms. (4) There is a shortage of priests in many areas today. (5) The infidelities and defections of priests are a scandal in the Church. (6) Celibacy is detrimental to the development of a mature well-balanced human personality. (7) A young man of twenty-five cannot make a free personal choice of celibacy, since he does not have sufficient knowledge or experience to make such a momentous decision.

The pope does not respond to these objections in order but touches on them *passim* in the course of his letter. He sets down at once the decision he has arrived at after prayer and reflection. He says: "We consider that the present law of celibacy should today continue to be firmly linked to ecclesiastical ministry." It is true, he notes, that the gift of celibacy is different from the gift of a priestly vocation; but it belongs to those who hold office in the Church to test and accept the vocation to the priesthood and to send into the ministry those candidates who are suitable and will best serve the community according to the conditions of time and place.

The pope then outlines the reasons or motives that appear to him to justify maintaining the law of celibacy. The reasons he appeals to are the Christological, ecclesiological and eschatological significance of a celibate priesthood.

By the Christological significance the pope

means that since the priests of the New Testament share in the priesthood of Christ and his role as mediator, they ought to reflect him in his ministry as closely as possible. This means that the priest ought to imitate him in the celibacy which indicated his singleminded dedication to the loving service of God and all men. The ecclesiological significance of a celibate clergy is the freedom and flexibility to dedicate oneself wholly and exclusively to the service of the kingdom. The eschatological significance consists in the sign of the presence on earth of the final stages of salvation and the stimulus to the pilgrim people to look forward and upward.

The pope then points to the ancient tradition in the Church, calling attention to the fact that neither in the West nor in the East are priests allowed to marry. This brief historical sketch culminates in a quotation from Pope John XXIII, in which he expressed his deep hurt that "anyone can dream" that the Church today will depart from this discipline.

However, Paul notes that there is the possibility of ordaining married men to the priesthood (i.e., Protestant ministers who become Catholics and want to exercise ministry in the Church) as well as to the diaconate. But, he adds, this is no prelude to the abolition of the present legislation which excludes those in sacred orders from marrying. He also adds that for very grave reasons and as a final measure dispensations will be given to priests and they will be allowed to return to the lay state. However, he reminds priests of their serious responsibility in petitioning a dispensation in view of the grave scandal that often occurs.

THE THEOLOGICAL ARGUMENT

In a discussion on clerical celibacy among seminarians, priests or sophisticated lay people I usually have found that anyone who takes a position defending mandatory celibacy fights a lonely battle. It is almost the "received doctrine" today that celibacy, while admittedly a great value, is a special charism and so should be made optional, accepted by those who have the charism but not imposed on everyone who experiences a call to ministry in the Church. After all, celibacy and priesthood are not necessarily connected; they are only connected juridically by canon law.

At this point I do not want either to reject or accept the conclusion of this argument. I do want to call attention to the fact that it leaves out one of the essentials. One factor is that celibacy and priesthood are not necessarily connected. Another is the practical reasons for maintaining or repealing the present legislation. The third factor, which is integral to the argument but often ignored, is the theological affinity that exists between celibacy and sacred orders. It is not enough and it does not do justice to the reality simply to say that there is no necessary connection. One must add that there is a strong affinity and it is only in the context of this affinity that the practical reasons can be weighed. Only when one understands and appreciates the affinity that exists between priesthood and celibacy is he in a position to evaluate rightly the more practical considerations. This is the point that is stressed in almost all theological literature on this topic.[4]

One of the most interesting and impassioned discussions of this question comes from Karl Rahner. It takes the form of an open letter to priests which is entitled "The Celibacy of the Secular Priest in Present-Day Conversation."[5] After an involuted beginning, Rahner gets to the point on the eighth page: celibacy is a theological question that cannot be adequately discussed in the abstract. Celibacy in general is seldom the question that bothers men; the question is rather about my celibacy, and rightly so. It is the way I realize my Christian faith, and it makes no difference that someone else may realize his faith differently. With this as a preface, Rahner gives the following personal statement of his own celibacy:

> Quite simply, I let go of a grand wonderful gift of this life because I believe in eternal life. . . .

Precisely when and in so far as the experience of the deep mystery of marriage has a long history, and when thereby the personal uniqueness of marriage and all its human interpersonal meaning—over and beyond all question of posterity and economic importance—becomes clearer today and in the future, then also the true nature of celibacy in its depths will appear more distinctly, and it will have very likely a future only among Christians . . . who believe in the Crucified. The wonderful, unfathomably tender and gentle gift of life, which is marriage, about which man knows, which a whole lifetime experiences always anew as such a gift, is given up in the believing hope of eternal life, and precisely in such a way that man knows that this eternal life remains a gift not only to this "I" but to all. Folly? Yes, the folly of the love of God and of faith in the death which alone gives *the* life.

Rahner rejects any accusation that he has fallen from theology into pious talk. For a man only knows the meaning of celibacy by experiencing it. He believes in the Gospel beforehand and then lives celibacy foolhardily, bravely believing that the Gospel knows what it is talking about. Besides, he says, there are different kinds of theology. The question we are dealing with here is "a chapter of theology which is not mastered at the desk of reasoning theology, nor in the talk of the majority, nor in the average conversation of a parish house. It remains a piece of kneeling and praying theology." And, he says, "I hope that this kind of theology is still had among us priests."

I think Rahner is quite right. Celibacy is a univocal term only if it is defined negatively—as abstention from marriage. When the term is given positive content it is realized somewhat differently in the uniqueness of each person. I can identify somewhat with what Rahner says but would describe my experience of my celibacy somewhat differently. In fact, I would describe my experience of celibacy somewhat differently than my theology of celibacy. I would not make my experience of celibacy my theology of celibacy, mainly because my experience of celibacy does not make as much sense, or rather does not make as much universal sense, as my theology of celibacy and therefore is much more vulnerable to criticism and attack by others. What further complicates the whole matter is, as Rahner points out, that "everybody lives in his decisions concretely from a knot of impulses and non-reflected motives." An articulation of one's experience will never be an altogether adequate description of one's preconceptual decision in the center of his subjectivity.

If I were asked to articulate my theology of priestly celibacy, I think I would adopt the view of Schillebeeckx: it is the result of an existential inability to do otherwise because of a consumption of one's energies in singleminded service of the kingdom. I would adopt this view partly because to some extent I identify with it, but mainly because I think it has more universal validity and is less vulnerable to attack than my own experience.

If, on the other hand, I were asked to articulate my own experience of celibacy, I would describe it as the result of a constant awareness that all the magnificence and beauty of this world is passing away and will end suddenly and abruptly in insubstantial ashes. It will do this at the end of time, or what is the same for me, at my death. What is more, nothing in this world can satisfy one's hunger for the infinite; only God can do that when he comes. This perception and awareness of the finitude of this world and all that is in it together with the expectation of the infinite in the next finds its expression in celibacy. This is for me the most authentic expression of who I am or at least of what is deepest in me. By freely abstaining from what I suspect is the best that can be had here—interpersonal love of a woman and the fathering of one's own sons and daughters—I can best express what is perhaps my most genuine and central experience of existence: a fundamental dissatisfaction with this world and a believing hope in the next. It is a question of where one's treasure is, there his heart is also.

Aside from what a psychiatrist might do with

this, it is also an inadequate theology, at least an inadequate universal theology. But I think that it justifies itself as long as it contains a part of a religious truth. No theological statement, not even a defined dogma, can do more than inadequately express part of a truth. If someone would say to me, "I do not identify with or accept your explanation of celibacy," I would reply, "I was talking about my celibacy not yours." In other words, I think Rahner is right when he suggests that we are dealing with more than any universal or abstract theology can bear. We are dealing with a highly personal charism, which will be realized in each individual in a highly personal way.

Rahner goes on to say that the Church can select for ministry to the community only those who have this charism or gift of celibacy. Because of the affinity or positive accord between ministry and celibacy, he believes that the traditional discipline should be maintained at almost any cost. He would even prefer moving the age of ordination back to thirty-five or later if that were ever proven necessary. He admits that the pastoral care of souls is of primary importance in the Church and celibacy of its clergy is secondary and that if there ever is a genuine shortage of priests in the Church as a whole or in some area the value of celibacy would have to yield to the primary value. But he is quick to point out that we must be very careful in how we define "shortage of priests." Perhaps the Holy Spirit is telling us something today by the decrease in vocations to the priesthood: so many tasks, even apostolic ones, that were performed by the clergy in the past really can and should be entrusted to the Christian laity.

Throughout his article Rahner shows himself if not cynical at least suspicious of the real motivation behind much of the present demand for marriage among the clergy: he does not think that it is inspired by faith and selfless love but by personal selfishness and the desire for one's own happiness. In regard to the future, he gives four personal opinions: (1) The Church should not and in fact will not abrogate the present law of celibacy. (2) She must improve the education of seminarians about the meaning of celibacy. (3) She should be largehearted in granting dispensations. (4) She may give the priesthood, as well as the diaconate, to married men.

I am inclined to agree with Rahner's prediction about the future of the law of celibacy. I suspect that in the not-too-distant future we will see the Church ordaining married men to both the diaconate and the priesthood. Dispensations from celibacy together with laicization will be granted more freely if not routinely. I cannot foresee the Church ever allowing priests to marry and retain the exercise of their office. As Schillebeeckx has pointed out, from the very earliest times until today, in both the East and the West, the Church has never done that. There have been pressures as great if not greater than there are today for the abolition of this discipline, but the rule has always and everywhere remained the same: no marriage after ordination. I do not expect that in the foreseeable future the Church will reverse that tradition. All things, of course, are possible, but what I am talking about is a prudent expectation or hope.

PRACTICAL CONCLUSIONS

Let us turn our thoughts to some practical consequences of all this. The first that occurs is that if it is true that there is no prudent hope of the Church allowing priests to marry, then the practical course for seminarians today is obvious. If I were a seminarian today and felt that I had a call to ministry but not to celibacy, my first course of action would be to pray to God for the gift of celibacy, believing that he is generous with his graces. If in the end I still did not feel that I also had a call to celibacy so that I could freely vow it before him, then I would leave the seminary and get married. This would be a painful decision, but it would be better than accepting sacred orders now with the hope that the law of celibacy will soon be changed, so that in five years or so I will be able to get married. We are dealing here with practical knowledge and prudent estimations. We have to live our lives in a world of probabilities. We cannot count on mere possibilities or make important decisions based on imprudent hopes. It is difficult enough to avoid making serious mistakes in life even when we remain hardheaded and realistic.

There does seem to be another possibility. If the Church does not change the law of celibacy within five or ten years, one could apply for a dispensation then and return to the state of a Christian layman. This plan deserves some comment. The Church does grant dispensations now and is likely to be even more lenient in the future. In the past the discipline was rigid and rigidly administered. When I was in the seminary we were told a story, which I suspect was spurious and something of an exaggeration, but did accurately reflect the mood of that period. According to the tale, a bishop wrote a petition to the Holy See asking for a dispensation from celibacy and laicization for one of his priests. He outlined all the grave reasons and argued that the priest's eternal salvation hung in the balance. He ended his letter with the words *ne pereat* ("lest he perish"). The Holy See answered the petition with one word: *Pereat* ("Let him perish"). Today a priest can be dispensed without too much trouble. There is no universal pattern, but ordinarily, with a minimum of red tape, a man can expect a favorable reply within six months.

There is no problem with this practice at the theoretical level. The commitment that a man makes at ordination is not an absolute one. It cannot be. Only an absolute being can effect something that is absolute. A vow is a promise about the future, but many of the contingencies of the future remain hidden from us. The Church or any human authority cannot make a law which binds absolutely in all possible situations precisely because a human authority cannot foresee all possible situations. Neither can an individual legislate for himself, as it were, in any absolute way. He will change in ways that he cannot foresee and so will his circumstances. Sometimes this change will result in a personal situation in which he cannot and should not remain a priest. If the Church did not grant dispensations from her law, I could imagine a situation in which an individual would not only be permitted but obliged to get married without a dispensation, making a prudent use of epikeia; for if there is a conflict between the good and the law, a man is bound always to the good, not to the law.

To say that the Church can, does and should give dispensations from celibacy after a man has committed himself to it at ordination and to say that no man can make a truly absolute commitment is not to tell the whole story. While the Church does grant dispensations *ex parte post* (after ordination), she still requires and expects a total, final, permanent commitment *ex parte ante,* that is, before ordination. It is essential to understand that while this commitment cannot be permanent in any absolute sense, it is permanent *humano modo,* in a truly human sense. To say that there are no absolute commitments among human beings is not to say that there are no commitments or that they are not truly commitments. Nor is it to say that none of them is in any sense final, permanent and binding. A promise is a promise and demands fidelity even though there may be extraordinary circumstances in which its binding force breaks down. It would certainly be inexcusably dishonest to feign this promise from the beginning, and wrong to go back on it when one encounters difficulties. Celibacy is not only a gift; it is also a task and a goal always still to be achieved.

A priest is obliged to celibacy by both a juridical bond and a moral commitment, and these two are not the same thing. The Church can dispense from the juridical bond but she cannot touch the moral commitment. That is between the individual and God. It is conceivable that a priest might go through all the proper legal channels and forms and be released from his juridical bond, with a smile and a warm handshake from his bishop, and still be guilty before God because of infidelity to his moral commitment. There are certainly good reasons why a priest may not be any longer obliged to his original moral commitment. So much so that he ought to leave the active priesthood and marry. But it would be a sign not of Christian charity but of heterodox doctrine to whitewash all cases automatically, as if there is never a sin involved. As someone recently remarked, the generals in Vietnam and Mayor Daley are not the only sinners in the world. Priests also can sin and one of the sins they can commit is infidelity to the commitment they made at ordination.

Because of the high moral value in a commitment Bernard Häring argues that a priest who rejects his celibacy should never be allowed to return to the active priesthood. He questions how, after having made a solemn promise in which he affirmed his knowledge of celibacy and his free acceptance of it, he could proclaim a morality of covenant, which is a morality of fidelity. A priest is not only a functionary; he is a witness of that which is at the heart of his message.[6]

The principal conclusion I draw from all this is that while there is no necessary connection between celibacy and ministry, there is a strong affinity, a positive accord, a suitability or fittingness. The reasons given for the affinity prove only that, not more. To object to them because they do not prove any necessary connection, because there is another way possible, is to misdirect one's aim and to confuse the argument. One can only listen to the reasons and through them try to estimate the strength and value of this affinity. Then, with an appreciation of this positive accord or suitability, and only then, can one rightly evaluate the practical reasons for maintaining or changing the Church law.

I would like to conclude by quoting this paragraph from Richard McCormick: "One would suspect that in this area we are more than ever liable to the inducements of an unrecognized utilitarianism. Celibacy participates in the mystery of Christ and in the folly of the cross in a way which at least partially resists analysis by theological argument and counterargument. Furthermore, as a form of witness, its effects are in the spiritual order and impervious to the type of empiricism we cling to so ardently. Does this not mean that the full value of celibacy is hard to come by? Does it not therefore mean that a judgment of the obsoleteness of a law requiring universal celibacy would be a very harrowing undertaking? I would not conclude from this that a conclusion of obsoleteness can never be drawn, or that it will not become clear one day that a celibate priesthood is a luxury we cannot afford. This is a possibility and we must remain open to it. I mean rather that there are value-factors about celibacy and a generally celibate priesthood which run rather deep. It is deceptively easy to be trigger-happy when discussing the usefulness or uselessness of a law which, drawing on these value-factors, prescribes celibacy for all priests."[7]

5. Contraception

THERE HAS been so much writing and talking about birth control in recent years that the whole topic has become tiresome. Although many of the discussions were highly emotional and polemic, some productive thinking was done, and now that some time has elapsed since *Humanae Vitae* and the furor of the debate has somewhat spent itself, perhaps we can begin calmly to sort out and distill some of the theological advances that have been made.

There can be no doubt that there are many good reasons why people should practice birth control. Respect for human life means respect for the quality of human life and not just its quantitative reproduction. Responsible parenthood means more than generous procreation. It also means the feeding, clothing, housing and education of children. Today in our society at least a high school education is necessary for a child if he is going to live with any dignity, and it is quite reasonable for parents to want to provide a college education for their sons and daughters. To fulfill the duties consequent upon procreation costs a large number of dollars.

The physical health of the mother is often an important consideration in deciding responsibly for or against another pregnancy. The nervous state and mental health of the contemporary suburban and urban housewife is increasingly important. Add the strains of modern life to the strain of raising children today and it is easy to see why there are women on every block who are nervous wrecks and many who already have been hospitalized for nervous breakdowns.

There is the larger problem of overpopulation. Many competent demographers and economists predict that within a few centuries the human race will be facing disaster. This prediction is challenged by other experts who think that the food problem can be solved by the use of fertilizers, tripling the present area of arable land, making food through photosynthesis of algae and most importantly by solving the real problem, which is not production but distribution of food. But even if the more optimistic experts are correct—and they may not be—even if technological man can prevent a demographic disaster for a number of centuries, the fact remains that many areas of the world are already suffering from starvation and crowding of human beings and that without birth control *now* human lives will continue to be dehumanized.

The Christian cannot be unconcerned about these things. He must always be engaged in making human life more human. But as he approaches these problems he ought to reflect for a moment on the ethical categories and principles he has in his head. His ethical presuppositions will largely determine the practical solution he comes to. Therefore these presuppositions ought to be checked for their soundness and conformity to the gospel.

One way that a Christian may approach the problem is with the tacit assumption that man is to be thought of primarily as Man the Citizen, living under law.[1] He is born in the midst of mores, laws and rules. As we carry on our scientific work under the laws of logic and scientific method, so we live our lives under the laws of right and wrong. Those who think of man as citizen believe that only right and lawful life is good and that lawful living is not a future ideal or good to be attained but an always present demand. When faced with the question, What shall I do? they raise as prior the question, What is right? What is the law?

Another way that a Christian may approach the

problem is with the tacit assumption that man is to be thought of primarily as Man the Maker, man the artisan, in pursuit of an ideal to be realized, a good to be attained, an end to be reached. In trying to answer the question, What shall I do? those who imagine man as maker raise as prior the question, What is my goal, ideal or end?

While both of these models—Man the Citizen and Man the Maker—are useful, neither is adequate and both can be misleading.

Working out of the model of Man the Citizen, Immanuel Kant came to a number of bizarre and obviously unchristian ethical conclusions. For instance, if a murderer wanted to kill your friend and chased him into your house and asked you if he was hiding somewhere in the house, you must answer him truthfully, saying, "Yes, he is hiding in that closet." You may not tell a lie. Only right and lawful life is good. In deciding what you should do you must ask, "What is the law?" and then conform to it. Kant did not waver in his conclusion even in this extreme case.[2] For what can be clearer than that Man the Citizen may never break the law? This is the image of man that inspired the defense of the German leaders at Nuremberg. They justified the most atrocious crimes by saying, "I was following orders." Millions of Jews had witnessed Man the Citizen doing his duty at Dachau and Buchenwald.

The other model or image of man, Man the

Maker, is also inadequate and so is dangerous if unilaterally taken to all its conclusions. It is the image of man that justified Nagasaki and Hiroshima. Man the Maker was in pursuit of peace and the saving of American lives. So he asked, "What is my goal?" and achieved it. The American conscience has been troubled ever since.

This relates directly to the problem of overpopulation. Among man's many goals there is hardly one more important than the survival of the human race. Many demographers tell us that this is precisely what is threatened by the population increase. Still, what Paul Ramsey said in connection with the predicted extinction of the race through genetic deterioration applies equally to the threat of extinction through overpopulation. He points out that

> when a Christian hears the gloomy prediction that a time will come when there will be no more like us to come after us, he will have to reply that he knew this all along. The Christian apocalypse in the Book of Revelation and Mark 13 and parallel passages tell us the same news in other rhetoric. The Christian already knows and believes that God means to kill us all in the end and in the end he is going to succeed. This does not mean that the Christian will be inactive or simply passively accept the . . . eventual extinction of the race. But it does mean that the Christian knows that he is not *bound* to succeed in prevent-

ing this any more than he is bound to hold up entropy or to prevent planets from colliding with the earth or to prevent the cooling of the sun. He knows of no absolute command of God to insure that this will not occur. This does not mean that he will do nothing. But it does mean that as he goes about the urgent business of doing his duty in regard to future generations he does not begin with the desired end as if it were an absolute value and deduce his obligations exclusively from this. He does not define what is good and right merely in terms of what is conducive to an absolutely imperative end. . . . He knows of no such absolutely imperative end that would justify any means, especially since this end is one of temporal history where success is not promised to mankind by either Scripture or sound reason.[3]

I will assume that infanticide, senicide, genocide, craniotomies and abortion are dehumanizing means of controlling birth.[4] If this is assumed, or the question at least set aside, we can turn our attention to the other techniques and means of birth control that are available.

METHODS OF CONTROLLING BIRTH[5]

A simple and common method of avoiding pregnancy without any mechanical devices or chemicals is the technique of Onan, *coitus interruptus* or withdrawal. Before ejaculation the man withdraws his penis from the vagina. There are a number of problems with this method. Intercourse before orgasm cannot be relaxed; it is frustrating for the man to withdraw at the very moment when his natural impulse is to drive his penis deeply into the vagina; the woman often does not reach orgasm; and since timing is so important, it is not always effective: the first few drops of ejaculate contain most of the spermatazoa; the secretion of the Cowper's glands sometimes contains sperm; and some sperm is left in the urethra after ejaculation so that reunion then would be dangerous. Withdrawal is considered to be between 92% and 60% effective in preventing conception, depending on the carefulness and timing of the man.

Another method is condomistic intercourse. A condom or "rubber" is a cone-shaped bag made of rubber or sheep's intestine. It is about an inch and one-half in diameter and about seven and one-half inches long. If it does not have a small pocket at the end to catch and hold the semen, the user should leave about a half inch loose at the end to prevent breakage. It also needs to be checked for holes before use either by blowing in it or preferably by filling it with water. About seven hundred and fifty million condoms are produced each year in the United States. They are used more frequently in non-marital intercourse and are very useful for the prevention of venereal disease. The condom does not dull pleasure appreciably unless it is coated with too much lubrication. There is always some danger of its breaking in use and of its slipping off or of semen trickling out after the penis becomes soft. In general, the condom is given a rating of about 89% effective in preventing conception.

There are two main types of contraceptive pessaries, the cervical cap and the diaphragm. The cervical cap is a metal, rubber or plastic cap that fits over the cervix and blocks the entrance of sperm into the uterus. It must be fitted by a physician and is kept in place partly by suction. It is generally used together with spermicidal creams or jellies. Since rubber caps can be worn for only twenty-four hours, most cervical caps are made of plastic; these can remain in during the whole time between menstrual periods. They are used more commonly in Europe than in the United States. They are difficult for the woman to insert and remove, and when left in place they sometimes have a tendency to migrate. They are about 96% to 90% effective.

The diaphragm is one of the most popular contraceptive devices in use today. Many women are returning to its use because of the scare about the pill or because of their own bad experience with the pill. The diaphragm is a piece of rubber stretched over a collapsible metal ring. It is inserted in the vagina so as to occlude the mouth of the uterus. It should be used together with spermicidal creams or jellies. It must be fitted the first time by a physician. After that the woman can learn to insert and remove it herself. It is inserted immediately or several hours before intercourse and may not be removed until about six hours afterwards. It may be left in place for as long as twenty-four hours. When used with spermicidal chemicals it is about 96% to 90% effective.

Another very effective instrument is the intra-uterine contraceptive device (IUCD). This is a small loop, spiral, bow or ring made out of plastic (or sometimes metal). It is inserted into the uterus and left there. A thin string attached to it hangs down through the vagina so that the woman can occasionally check to see if it is still in place. How precisely it prevents pregnancy is not entirely clear. Some few medical authorities think that it causes peristalsis of the fallopian tubes so that the released ovum travels through the tubes and uterus too quickly to be fertilized. What appears to be the case is that it interferes with nidation. In some way it renders the complex process of implantation impossible, hence its effect is contraimplantation rather than contraception. It might therefore be classified as an abortifacient rather than as a contraceptive device.[6] Although it sometimes causes bleeding and pain and sometimes is rejected by the uterus, it is so simple, cheap and effective that Dr. Guttmacher predicts that it will be the most important contraceptive for the immediate foreseeable future. It is rated between 99% and 97% effective.[7]

Spermicidal chemicals are also used. They generally come in the form of creams, jellies and foams. Sometimes vaginal suppositories which melt after about fifteen minutes or vaginal tablets which dissolve in moisture are used. These chemicals must be inserted into the vagina from five to fifteen minutes before ejaculation occurs. They are considered to be between 95% to 73% effective. The new foams in aerosol spray cans are easily spread all around the vagina and are between 97% to 90% effective.

Vaginal douches are relatively ineffectual and are rated only about 64% effective. The vagina is flushed out after intercourse with plain water or some solution like vinegar, soapsuds or alum. Other devices sometimes used, such as sponges, tampons or balls of cotton treated with spermicides, are also relatively ineffective. Their rating is about 73% to 68%.

The most effective means is sterilization. The male can be sterilized by a simple surgical operation performed under local anesthesia in the physician's office. It is called a vasectomy. An incision is made on both sides in the scrotum above the testicles and an inch of the vas deferens is excised and the two ends are tied. Since no more sperm will be carried to the seminal vesicles and those already present will die after a short time, fertility will come to an end after several days. After the operation the man is not incapacitated but should avoid strenuous work or exercise for about two days. If the operation is done skillfully spontaneous recanalization rarely takes place. The man normally suffers no impotency or decrease of sexual desire. Two hundred thousand vasectomies are performed each year in the United States and the procedure should become more widespread as some of the myths that surround it are laid to rest. If for some reason a man regrets his decision, it is sometimes possible to repair the vasectomy. Today there is about a 50% chance of success in an attempt to restore fertility through surgical recanalization of the tubes.

Castration, the surgical removal of the testicles, is a more drastic method of sterilization. It often results in changes in secondary sex characteristics, which however can be controlled by hormone therapy. It does not necessarily result in impotence if it is performed on an adult. But if one's only purpose is sterilization, a vasectomy is the preferred technique today.[8]

Surgical sterilization of the female is a complicated procedure. There are four techniques currently in use. An oophorectomy is the surgical excision of both ovaries. After the ovaries are removed no more ova are produced, and hormone therapy is sometimes needed to prevent changes in secondary sex characteristics. A salpingectomy is a major surgical operation in which the abdomen is opened and the fallopian tubes are cut, tied and resectioned. It is easily done and often recommended by doctors during a Caesarean section. The operation requires a recuperative period of four to five days and is considered about 99% effective or better in preventing pregnancy. An attempt may later be made to rejoin the tubes so as to restore fertility, but the operation is risky and the chance of success is small. Work is presently in progress on a simpler technique in which metal or plastic clamps are attached to the tubes by way of a small incision in the vagina.

A technique which is used frequently in Japan and probably will receive more attention in the United States is intrauterine coagulation of the uterine tube outlet. The openings of the tubes into the uterus are electrically cauterized and as a result scar tissue forms and permanently blocks the tubular orifices.

A hysterectomy, i.e., the surgical removal of the uterus, is generally performed through the vagina. It is seldom performed solely for the purpose of sterilization.

Birth control pills are probably best classified as

sterilizing drugs, since sterilization is their primary effect, although they also seem to work as contraceptives and abortifacients. The pills are a combination of synthetic hormones (progesterone and estrogen) which does three things: (1) it inhibits the production of pituitary gonadotropin and so inhibits the growth and development of the ovarian follicles (sterilization); (2) it affects the mucous lining of the uterus so as to make implantation more difficult and early spontaneous abortion more likely if conception does take place (abortion); and (3) it causes the mucous plug of the cervix to thicken so as to keep sperm from entering the uterus (contraception).

A woman starts taking the pills on the fifth day after the first day of menstruation. She takes one each day, preferably at the same hour, for twenty days. Menstruation will usually start again two to five days after the last pill is taken. Five days after the menstruation begins she starts the cycle of pills again, and so on until she no longer wishes to be infertile. If menstruation does not occur after her twenty pills, she simply begins taking them again after seven days. When taken according to instructions oral contraceptives are practically 100% effective in preventing a pregnancy.

Some women cannot or do not want to take the pill because they suffer annoying or painful side effects, such as gastrointestinal disturbances, weight gain, headaches, spotting and irregular bleeding, cramps and painful swelling of the breasts. If the pills are taken steadily over a long period of time (one and one-half to three years), the woman's sex drive is reduced. Also, if she is taking the pill she generally cannot or should not try to nurse a child; milk production may be suppressed by the pill or hormones may pass into a baby boy's bloodstream which will have a feminizing effect on him.

The pill, of course, is often prescribed for therapeutic purposes other than the suppression of fertility, for instance as a remedy for premenstrual tension, excessive bleeding, an irregular menstrual cycle and certain skin disorders.

Another method of controlling birth is abstaining from sexual intercourse during the fertile days of the month. This is known as the safe period or rhythm method. A woman generally ovulates about once a month. The ovum lives about twenty-four hours after ovulation and the sperm can live in the uterus for about forty-eight hours. Therefore conception is possible only during three days of the month.

Ovulation is generally believed to take place fourteen to sixteen days before menstruation. Therefore to determine the time of ovulation a woman must count back from the first day of her next anticipated menstruation. By counting back sixteen days she arrives at the earliest time of ovulation, and by counting back fourteen days she arrives at the latest time of ovulation. If she has a twenty-eight-day menstrual cycle, she will ovulate between the thirteenth and fifteenth day after the first day of her period. Allowing for the life span of the ovum and sperm, she should abstain from coitus from the eleventh to the seventeenth day after the first day of her last menstruation.

If a woman has an irregular menstrual cycle, she should keep written records of the time of menstruation during a year, so as to determine the earliest and the latest time of menstruation. For instance, if her cycle varies between twenty-four and twenty-eight days, by counting back sixteen from the earliest time of the next menstruation and fourteen from the latest time of the next menstruation she can determine the earliest time of ovulation (eight days after the first day of the last period) and the latest time of ovulation (fifteen days after the first day of the last period). Adding time for the viability of the sperm and egg, she can determine that conception will be possible between the sixth and seventeenth days after the beginning of her menstrual period.[9]

Aside from the emotional or psychological difficulties that sometimes result from abstinence during the fertile or unsafe period, there are also some technical problems with this method. Certain emotions, such as fear or joy, can postpone or hasten ovulation. After childbirth the first few months are frequently too irregular for any safe period to be calculated, and during menopause the menstrual cycle is generally too irregular to permit reliable calculations of fertile periods. About 15% of women have too irregular a cycle to use this method at all.

Another method of determining the time of ovulation is by measurement of basal temperature, or lowest normal body temperature of the day. At the time of ovulation or one or two days after there is a dip in temperature and then a sharp rise of one-half to seven-tenths of a degree; the temperature remains at this higher level until one or two days before the beginning of the next period. Since the ovum lives only for one or two days, after this rise in temperature no conception is possible for the rest of that cycle. A woman should keep a record of her temperature in the morning for about six months to determine any peculiarities. One of the problems with this method is that other factors, such as a cold, can cause a rise in temperature and so confuse the pattern. Also, it is possible for more than one ovum to mature during a cycle.

Because of the polemics that have surrounded the question of rhythm or periodic continence as the "Catholic" method of birth control, it is difficult to ascertain how effective it really is. Some authorities rate it as 86% effective; others make higher claims. Mary S. Calderone, M.D., the medical director of the Planned Parenthood Federation of America, Inc., said this: "Stop apologizing for the rhythm method. We have a tendency to . . . list all of the medical methods, and then say, with a shrug, 'and the rhythm method.' Well, we should know the facts about it: it is very effective. . . . You're going to have failures with practically any method, but you are certainly going to have failures with the rhythm method, not because it is not effective, but because the restrictions it places on people make it rate low in acceptability."[10]

For the record we might note another method known as Carezza, or as it is called in most of the moral literature, *amplexus reservatus*. This is the prolongation of coitus, even for hours, without male ejaculation. It does not seem to have gained much popularity.[11]

THE THEOLOGICAL ARGUMENT

Since *Humanae Vitae* the principal theological question has shifted. What began as an argument in moral theology has become a larger and more important problem of ecclesiology. In the next chapter we will shift our attention to the ecclesiological question and the related problem of the practical formation of conscience. In the pages that remain here it will be enough to outline the principal theological arguments about the morality of artificial birth control.

The argument made against contraception by Pope Paul in *Humanae Vitae* is the same as that made in the recent past by such theologians as Josef Fuchs and Richard McCormick. Fuchs, of course, changed his opinion during the study and discussions of the papal birth control commission and expressed his revised opinion in the majority report. I am not sure what his opinion is after *Humanae Vitae,* since he issued no public statement. McCormick currently does not reject the traditional teaching as certainly erroneous or clearly inadequate, but he does think that even after *Humanae Vitae* it is subject to solid and positive doubt.[12] One sees a lot of caution among good theologians even as they move from one theological opinion to another.

The principal ethical argument against contraception is based on an analysis of the act of sexual intercourse as an expression of a love relationship which is total self-giving and procreative in character. Fuchs developed the argument in this way:

> The Creator so arranged the sexual act that it is simultaneously both per se generative and per se

expressive of intimate oblative love. He has so arranged it that procreation would take place from an act intimately expressive of conjugal love and that this act expressive of conjugal love would tend toward procreation. Therefore an act which *of itself* does not appear to be apt for procreation is by this very fact shown to be one which does not conform to the intentions of the Creator. The same thing should be said about an act which *of itself* is not apt for the expression of oblative love. Indeed, an act which is not apt for procreation is by this very fact shown to be one which is *of itself* not apt for the expression of conjugal love; for the sexual act is one.[13]

This is the same argument that found its way into *Humanae Vitae,* where Pope Paul wrote:

That teaching, often set forth by the magisterium, is founded upon the inseparable connection, established by God and unable to be broken by man on his own initiative, between the unitive and procreative meanings, both of which are present in the conjugal act. For by this intimate structure, the conjugal act, while most closely uniting husband and wife, also capacitates them for the generation of new life, according to laws inscribed in the very being of man and woman. By safeguarding both of these essential aspects, the unitive and the procreative, the use of marriage preserves in its fullness the sense of true mutual love and its ordination to man's exalted calling to parenthood.[14]

Both the strength and the weakness of this argument are pointed up in the approach of Paul Ramsey. Ramsey affirms that sexual intercourse is at the same time an act of love and a procreative act. By this he does not mean that it always in fact nourishes love and engenders a child but that it tends of its own nature toward strengthening of love (the unitive good) and engendering of children (the procreative good). This affirmation is not based on natural law in the sense of the mere fact and function of biological life, but on the Christian story of creation which appears not in the Book of Genesis but in the Prologue of St. John's Gospel and in Ephesians 5. Here we see that God created the entire world of his creatures out of love: God's love was creative and he created nothing apart from his love. Human love is made in the image of God's love. Human love reflects God's love because it is procreative. We procreate new beings like ourselves in the midst of our love for one another. In this there is a trace of the original mystery by which God created the world because of his love. Therefore God's love is normative for Christian love. Hence a couple may not "procreate from beyond their marriage, or exercise love's one-flesh unity outside of it."[15]

Notice Ramsey's conclusion. He argues that man may not radically put asunder what God has joined together; but God made human love procreative. Therefore, Ramsey concludes, not that contraception is illicit (that is what the pope concludes), but that artificial insemination and fornication are illicit, since by artificial insemination one procreates beyond the sphere of mutual love, and by fornication one loves beyond the sphere of responsible procreation. But by contraception the spheres of love and procreation are not separated, even though the act as unitive and procreative is divided.

The Catholic thesis, however, wants to conclude more from the premises. It wants to conclude that each act is unitive and procreative by God's design. Speaking of the separability of these two aspects of coitus as it has been defended by non-Catholics, Fuchs argued: "They do not sufficiently grasp that the Creator *united* this double aspect. The sexual faculty has but *one* natural actuation in which the generative and oblative aspects specify each other."[16] McCormick contended that contraceptive interference cannot be viewed as a merely biological intervention. Rather, contraception does not permit the act to be procreative and *therefore* it does not permit the act to be expressive of personal love, either because it expresses some restriction in self-donation or because the permanent sign of this love, the child, is excluded. In other words, the marital act is essentially an act of procreative love. This is the act as given to us by God. If the married couple are to use it properly, they must allow the act to retain both of these essential characteristics.

In the past few years many theologians, including Fuchs and McCormick, have found this analysis difficult to sustain. It is not easy to see why it is not sufficient to conclude, as Ramsey does, that one may not separate the unitive and procreative goods in principle but that separation is possible in an individual act. There are many acts of coitus that are in fact sterile and yet are expressive of personal love.

The central affirmation of *Humanae Vitae* is that each marriage act must remain open to the transmission of life and therefore every act of contraceptive intercourse is intrinsically evil. I think that it is fair to say that on the level of ethical analysis this affirmation remains unproven.

6. Humanae Vitae and Personal Conscience

IMMEDIATELY AFTER the release of *Humanae Vitae* a group of theologians from the Catholic University of America and elsewhere issued a public statement of dissent; they said: "It is common teaching in the Church that Catholics may dissent from authoritative, non-infallible teachings of the magisterium when sufficient reasons for doing so exist. Therefore, as Roman Catholic theologians . . . we conclude that spouses may responsibly decide according to their conscience that artificial contraception in some circumstances is permissible and indeed necessary to preserve and foster the values and sacredness of marriage."[1]

In a long letter to the *National Catholic Reporter* Charles Meyer wrote in response: "As their major premise [these theologians] place the proposition that it is the common teaching of the church that Catholics may dissent from authoritative but non-infallible teachings of the magisterium when sufficient reasons for doing so exist. This is, *salva reverentia,* not quite true. Common teaching holds that those who are *experts* in the field may withhold their assent while they propose to the proper authorities reasons which *have not yet been considered* by the magisterium in reaching its decision."[2]

Meyer, of course, is quite right. According to traditional theological teaching, the only one who was not required to give internal intellectual assent to the doctrine of *Humanae Vitae* was an expert in the field who had come across some new evidence that was not available to and considered by the magisterium. Even then, he was not to dissent publicly but simply to bring the new evidence he had discovered to the attention of the Holy See. Therefore the theologians' statement that individual Catholic couples had the freedom to form their own consciences contrary to papal teaching was a new and bold opinion, not the common traditional one. To say that it is new is not to say that it is false, but it does seem to demand that it be subjected to some careful theological scrutiny and analysis before it is accepted.

The phrase *freedom of conscience* has already become a cliché, and the idea that it conveys has almost become a dogma in certain Catholic circles. This is remarkable because the phrase is of such recent coinage and had no previous currency in Catholic theological history. Even in the Second Vatican Council's *Declaration on Religious Freedom* neither the phrase nor the idea appears. In fact, it was the intention of the bishops of the Council, following the express wish of Pope Paul, to distinguish carefully between two quite different freedoms, the religious freedom of a citizen within society and the freedom of a Catholic within the Church. In endorsing freedom of religion as a principle in the civil order, the Council simply affirmed a person's immunity from external coercion in society. On the other question—that of freedom of conscience within the Church—it said, near the end of the document: "In the formation of their consciences, the Christian faithful ought carefully to attend to the sacred and certain doctrine of the Church. The Church is, by the will of Christ, the teacher of the truth. It is her duty to give utterance to, and authoritatively to teach, that Truth which is Christ Himself, and also to declare and confirm by her authority those principles of the moral order which have their origin in human nature itself."[3]

I do not think that it is the intent of this statement to deny freedom of conscience. Rather, it simply sets it off as a separate question. In a note on this text, John Courtney Murray said that this document "will be a stimulus for the articulation of a full theology of Christian freedom in relation to the doctrinal and disciplinary authority of the Church." While awaiting the full articulation of this theology, I offer the following analysis. Our main interest here, in connection with *Humanae Vitae,* is the freedom of the Catholic conscience vis-à-vis the doctrinal authority of the Church. Since my analysis associates this with the freedom of conscience before the disciplinary authority of the Church, it will be necessary to consider this latter question first.

FREEDOM OF CONSCIENCE

The sense attributed to "freedom of conscience" by nineteenth-century continental laicism cannot be taken seriously by any Christian. Conscience cannot be conceived as absolutely autonomous, as making up for itself rather than discerning the true moral good and the binding will of God. This form of subjectivism is epistemologically as well as theologically untenable and no Christian theologian holds it today. Some Protestant theologians, including Paul Lehmann and H. R. Niebuhr, emphasize the necessity of avoiding the kind of individualism that would make conscience a god. According to these theologians, the Christian conscience is neither exclusively heteronomous nor autonomous. It is better described as theonomous and contextual. While it is not formed in the individual by ecclesiastical authority or by any other person than himself, neither is it a law unto iself, a creator of the moral good. God's will is always normative for it, and this will is not found solipsistically but in a Christian context, that is to say in a *koinonia,* a community engaged in conversation.

Catholics will agree that God's will can more safely be found in an ecclesial context. But at this point the Catholic notion of Church gives rise to a difference, because for a Catholic the ecclesial context includes a juridical authority. The practical importance of this juridical authority in the day-to-day lives of Catholics can easily be exaggerated. Sometimes people are simply too timid to exercise the freedom that they have. Lay people, priests and even bishops are sometimes afraid to make a decision that is properly theirs to make; so they appeal to ecclesiastical superiors to make it for them. What is more, Karl Rahner has reminded us that there are vast areas of our moral life that the Church does not and cannot regulate. The Church has no competence to determine by law whether a particular girl should enter the convent, join the Peace Corps, go to graduate school or marry Tom, Dick or Harry.

Humanae Vitae *and Personal Conscience*

The Church cannot dictate by precept whether a certain man should become a doctor, lawyer, merchant or chief, whether he should belong to this union or not, vote for this political candidate or against him, work to establish this concrete political, economic, legal or educational system, use these particular weapons in this particular war and so forth. Many ethical decisions so depend on the singular concrete elements of a unique situation that they cannot be deduced from universal principles and therefore cannot be regulated by universal laws. And yet existential moral decisions of this sort are often the most important and far-reaching that a man will be called upon to make in his lifetime.

All of this obviously does not obscure the fact that the Church does make laws and issue precepts that are binding on Catholics. But the individual, in giving obedience to legitimate authority, cannot abstain from judging about his own actions. He cannot mechanically obey the law made by legitimate authority as if the law will always and necessarily prescribe the true moral good and proscribe the genuine moral evil. Laws made by legitimate authority are not necessarily and automatically good. Certain legal norms may exist at a given moment in history for a variety of reasons. One may be that they are useful or necessary for the common good. However, one cannot exclude a priori the possibility that the principal reason for the existence of a certain law at a certain time is the legislator's inertia, ignorance, self-interest or cowardice before external pressures. One does not presume these motives, but he cannot abstain from judging, as if nothing else were required of him but mechanically to obey the law. The experiences in Nazi Germany have brought home clearly that one cannot take refuge in the fact that he followed orders. Each of us is responsible for his own actions. He must make his own judgment about his actions and it is this judgment that he must follow in the end.

Even the best laws cannot provide for every situation. Positive laws, St. Thomas tells us, bind *in pluribus;* they provide for normal situations, not for all of them. The individual conscience must judge whether a law obliges in a particular situation. It is significant that St. Thomas, unlike Suarez, did not understand epikeia as a way to get out of moral obligations. He saw it as a virtue by which a man applies the law to his situation in a way that contradicts the words of the law. A man is obliged to do more than merely fulfill the letter of positive laws. He is obliged to seek out and perform the true moral good in each situation. If in a particular situation the general law is in conflict with the genuine good, a man is obliged to the good not to the law. Epikeia, therefore, is not merely a device to escape obligations or to lighten the burdens of law. It is a Christian virtue which, like any other virtue, can be sinned against. The Christian is called to responsible situational decisions and choices, not to the mechanical observance of laws.

Freedom of conscience vis-à-vis the disciplinary authority of the Church does not mean that a man tempers the tyranny of authority with his own insubordination. Nor does it mean that he obeys the legitimate commands of authority only when he himself happens to agree with them. Even less does it mean the freedom to do whatever one pleases. It means rather the freedom and duty to do always and only what I myself think is right. The laws of legitimate authority are normative for the Christian, but they are not always applicable. To judge their binding force and relevance in one's own situation is the burden and freedom of conscience.

This brings us to the question of the freedom of the Catholic conscience before the doctrinal or teaching authority of the Church. Since it does not pertain to the question of *Humanae Vitae,* we can separate out and prescind from the special problem of dogmatic definitions of faith and inquire directly into the question of the freedom of the individual Catholic conscience in relation to the authentic non-infallible magisterium. The problem is posed sharply by these words from the Second Vatican Council's *Constitution on the Church:* "In matters of faith and morals, the bishops speak in the name of Christ and the faithful are to accept their teaching and adhere to it with a religious assent of soul. This religious submission of will and of mind must be shown in a special way to the authentic teaching authority of the Roman Pontiff, even when he is not speaking *ex cathedra*. That is, it must be shown in such a way that his supreme magisterium is acknowledged with reverence, the judgments made by him are sincerely adhered to, according to his manifest mind and will."[4]

This statement, of course, says nothing new. The same doctrine was already taught by Pius XII in *Humani Generis* and by Pius XI in *Casti Connubii* and is found more or less clearly in numerous ecclesiastical documents at least from the time of Pius IX. And, it might be useful to notice, it is itself only authentic non-infallible teaching.

In the Spring, 1968, issue of *Chicago Studies* George Malone called attention to a then recent statement of Bishop Carlo Colombo. Writing in *Seminarium* the bishop said that if the theologian's research reveals that some authentic magisterial teaching is inadequate or erroneous, he can and should withdraw his assent to it and propose his reasons in order to aid the entire Church. As Charles Meyer pointed out, the older manualists also taught that in a rare case an expert could licitly suspend interior assent to authentic teaching in certain very special circumstances. The specific casuistry engaged in by the traditional authors is quite different from the sweeping statement that individual Catholics may dissent for sufficient reason and follow their own consciences rather than papal teaching. We will be able to illuminate this difference if we look beyond the specific casuistry of the traditional opinion and try to identify in it the underlying principle permitting dissent.

There are two reasons why a Catholic is obliged to give assent to authentic non-infallible teaching. One is that such assent is dictated by prudence: the presumption is in favor of the authentic teacher rather than the individual Christian. The other is that the assent is required by religious obedience: the authentic teacher has authority from Christ to bind the consciences of Christians in religious matters. After citing St. Pius X's teaching that one who impugns authentic magisterial decisions is guilty of both temerity and disobedience,[5] Van Noort notes: "The will can prudently order the assent because there is a legitimate presumption that the authentic teacher is not making a mistake; furthermore, the will is attracted to order the assent by the obligation of subjection towards the magisterium established by Christ and, consequently, from a motive of religious obedience."[6]

It is easy to see that neither of these reasons is absolute or unexceptional. The presumption is in favor of the magisterium, but presumptions yield to truth. The presumption in favor of the authentic fallible decrees of the magisterium is weighty but not so weighty that it cannot be weakened or overcome by serious reasons.

The other factor requiring assent to authentic teaching is religious obedience. The Christian owes obedience to legitimate authority, and the teaching Church has the authority from God to command the faithful to accept with their minds certain doctrinal propositions. This motive brings us back into the juridical order of Church discipline. Here, of course, the virtue of epikeia is operative. A Catholic is bound to obey but not to obey mechanically. He is first bound to judge and in the end to do only and always what he himself thinks is right. When the precept commands one to assent to a statement, to think that it is true, the binding force of this precept in a concrete situation is still subject to the judgment of conscience. A man must also think only and always what he himself thinks is true.

What we have been looking for is a principle relating freedom of conscience to authentic magisterial authority, and it seems to come to this: The individual Christian conscience has the same kind of freedom before authentic non-infallible teaching as it does before Church law. This is not the kind of freedom that escapes external objective norms. Magisterial teaching is normative for the Catholic conscience: it is presumably true and generally binding. That is not to say that it is necessarily true or binding in every situation. To decide on other objective grounds the situational validity of authentic fallible teaching is the burden and freedom of conscience.

This principle applies universally, and it is doubtful whether any more detailed or specific casuistry can be worked out with any success. It seems to me that it is not possible to sustain the more specific casuistry found in the common traditional theology of dissent. For instance, this theology requires for legitimate dissent that the dissenter be a professional theologian who is an expert in the field. It is, of course, a useful caution to remind us that reasonable dissent requires that one is informed and knows what he is talking about. It is also true that the presumption is that an expert or a theologian is more likely to be informed than is an ordinary Catholic couple. But it does not follow nor can it be set up as a principle that only the theological expert can be sufficiently informed. In such moral matters as birth control, the magisterium, the professional theologian and the lay Christian can have access to the same basic evidence.

We are in a very treacherous area of conscience

here. The temptation is strong in most of us to attach too much importance and weight to our own arguments and opinions. This common temptation is probably the reason the older authors cautioned that the legitimate denial of religious assent will occur very rarely. It is true that it will occur as an exception to the general rule, but it is doubtful that the frequency of the exception can be determined a priori. Only historical evidence can reveal how often authentic teaching has been wrong in the past and therefore give some indication of the strength of the presumption in its favor.

The traditional teaching also maintained that dissent was legitimate only if based on new evidence not known and considered by the authentic magisterium. But does this not assume that the magisterium will necessarily judge correctly about the evidence it has? Does not this exclude a priori the possibility that the principal reason for the magisterium's decision might be inertia, ignorance, misunderstanding, self-interest or cowardice before external pressures? One does not presume these motives, but he cannot abstain from judging.

The old opinion also required that the dissenter propose his doubt and the new evidence prompting it to the Holy See privately and quietly. It is quite true that any dissent from papal teaching demands humility and that one should avoid even the appearance of setting himself up as a competing magisterium. In many instances the private confidential manifestation of dissent might well be the only prudent way of proceeding and be demanded by the common good of the Church. But one cannot exclude the alternative, namely public dissent, which might be more useful in certain situations. It was Pope Pius XII, not the editors of the *National Catholic Reporter,* who first called to our notice the need for public opinion in the Church. It is precisely public opinion, created through public dissent, that in certain circumstances can best offset and eventually undo erroneous teaching.

APPLICATION TO *Humanae Vitae*

It is my conclusion that any Catholic has the fundamental right to dissent privately and sometimes even publicly from the authoritative non-infallible teaching of the official magisterium. This does not, of course, imply that all dissent is correct and without any fault. The dissent must be based on solid reasons. If the dissent of any individual is uninformed or based on ignorance it cannot be defended. It is also true that the decision most people come to on the question of contraception is not disinterested. One must always be on guard against a dishonest conclusion, one that is prejudiced by selfish motivation. As Richard McCormick has pointed out,

> Christian thought is now, as it always has been, a child of its times. Far more than a Christian, be he layman or theologian, can reflexly grasp, his culture is the soil which nourishes and subtly influences his thought. This has to scare us. For contemporary Western culture appears to be pansexualized to almost incredible depths. . . . Therefore a generous purchase on a self-questioning humility is in order for any realistic theologian as he weighs the importance of his own reflections in the area of human sexuality at this time in history. Secondly, anyone who reads the current literature on *Humanae Vitae* cannot help but notice that articles favoring the papal teaching manifest a heavy, almost exclusive concern with tradition and authority. Those which dissent are concerned largely with the analysis of evidence and reasoning. Obviously both aspects are important in Christian moral thought. But their relationship is still an uneasy and fragile thing in the Catholic community, especially at a time of escalating cultural antagonism to authority in general.[7]

Honesty in one's effort to come to a conscientious conclusion about contraception requires that one place under careful scrutiny his own attitude toward ecclesiastical and magisterial authority. It is certainly bad theological methodology to go from the conclusion that the immorality of contraception is not infallibly taught to the presumption that it is therefore erroneous. One does not start with this presumption about authentic non-infallible teaching but rather with the opposite.

The question remains: What about the teaching of *Humanae Vitae* that every contraceptive act is objectively sinful? Are there sufficiently solid reasons for the individual Catholic to dissent honestly from this teaching in the formation of his own conscience?

There are basically two reasons that led to the decision of *Humanae Vitae*. One is the natural law argument which we analyzed in the preceding chapter. The other is the argument from tradition, which is not properly a philosophical but an ecclesiological argument.

As I indicated, it is not easy to understand how the Holy Father could get the necessary certitude and clarity from the argument from reason. It is true that we must be wary, especially in moral matters, of the kind of rationalism that expects too much certitude from human reason. But neither can we assume that the pope gets his knowledge in some magical way. The pope's teaching is not merely as good as the arguments he uses, nor is it independent of these arguments. The fact that a pope teaches a doctrine as true is itself a weighty argument in its favor, but it does not overcome all arguments and reason, nor does it preclude error or rule out dissent. Because of the limitations of the natural law argument, McCormick, after six months' reflection, expressed his own doubt about the doctrine of *Humanae Vitae*. In his "Notes on Moral Theology" he concluded:

> In the light of these reflections it is the opinion of the compositor of these Notes that the intrinsic immorality of every contraceptive act remains a teaching subject to solid and positive doubt. This is not to say that this teaching of *Humanae Vitae* is certainly erroneous. It is only to say that there are very strong objections that can be urged against it and very little evidence that will sustain it. One draws this conclusion reluctantly and with no small measure of personal anguish. With proper allowance made for one's own shortcomings, pride, and resistance, what more can a theologian say? He can say, of course, that the teaching is clear and certain simply because the papal magisterium has said so. But ultimately such an assertion must rest on the supposition that the clarity and certainty of a conclusion of natural-law morality are independent of objective evidence.[8]

The other argument that led to the conclusion of *Humanae Vitae* was not a philosophical but a properly theological or more specifically an ecclesiological one. It is true that the immorality of contraception was not defined infallibly in the papal encyclical, and that is the reason it is said to be authentic non-infallible teaching. But this fact by itself does not establish the theological note of the doctrine. The fact that the pope did not make use of his extraordinary magisterium and infallibly define the doctrine in his encyclical letter does not mean that it is not infallible doctrine. It is possible that it is infallible doctrine on another count, that is to say *ex ordinario magisterio*. A particular doctrine may be infallibly taught by the bishops throughout the world exercising their ordinary magisterium without being infallibly taught by the pope exercising his extraordinary magisterium. No pope in Catholic history has ever infallibly defined a matter of morality, and so it is no surprise that Pope Paul did not infallibly define the immorality of contraception, since there is no precedent in history for that procedure. The point I am trying to make—which is not sufficiently clarified in many of the popular discussions of this question—is that a serious attempt to ascertain the weight or importance of the theological tradition does not end with the assertion that *Humanae Vitae* is authentic non-infallible teaching.

Although this may be true on the theoretical level, as soon as one tries to determine the theological note of this doctrine he finds that it is practically impossible. A survey of the literature reveals that the opinions vary from infallibly defined to merely authentic non-infallible teaching. At one extreme Gregory Baum holds that natural law precepts are not an object of infallibility, since they are derived from human wisdom not revelation. At the other pole are Felix Cappello, Arthur Vermeersch and others who say that the doctrine is defined *ex cathedra* and infallibly by Pope Pius XI in *Casti Connubii*. Many authors claim that the doctrine is infallibly taught by the bishops exercising their ordinary magisterium; others hold that it is proximate to faith and definable and irreformable doctrine; and others do not address the question at all.

Before one decides that the Catholic Church's teaching on contraception is erroneous he ought to weigh carefully the conservatives' principal argument, which was expressed by Ford and Kelly in these words: "If the teaching of the Catholic Church on a point so profoundly and intimately connected with the salvation of millions of souls has been the same over such a long period of time, the inevitable conclusion must be that that teaching is true and unchangeable. Otherwise the Church which God established to interpret the moral law and to guide souls on the way of salvation would be failing substantially in its divine mission."[9] In other words, as Noonan's study has shown, the Church's teaching on contraception has been always and everywhere the same.[10] Bishops, preachers, catechisms and confessors have insisted on the immorality of contraception. Even if they did not teach it in a way that demands the technical note of infallible doctrine (and even this point is arguable), they did teach it as the true and certain will of God and denied the sacraments to all who did not follow it. What kind of Church have we and where is the Spirit who is supposed to guard it from error? Does the Spirit protect the magisterium from universal error in relatively insignificant matters like the Assumption of Mary and desert her through her whole history until now on a point so profoundly and intimately connected with the salvation of millions of souls?

This is the heart of the whole problem. I think it is fair to say, with Robert Springer, that the issue is no longer contraception. The problem is whether an error of such gravity and without any comparable historical precedent is compatible with the Catholic Church's self-image. Can the possibility of such an error be assimilated by Catholic ecclesiology?

The replies that argue that the natural law in this matter has changed or that the previous teaching of the Church was historically conditioned are not satisfactory. It is true that natural law can change and that the Church's teaching is often if not always historically conditioned. But I do not think that these two facts have application to the matter of contraception in a way that solves the problem. Bruno Schüller is quite right when he says: "The much talked of and doubtless real necessity of situating magisterial judgments in their historical context should never be used to pronounce as correct a priori some of those judgments which seem to us today to be false. Pushed to its extreme, this could result in historical relativism—a much worse position than that involved in admitting an error of the magisterium."[11]

A more honest and direct response to the problem was given by the majority on the papal birth control commission when they said that the criteria for determining what the Spirit can or cannot permit in the Church cannot be determined a priori. We must look at the kinds of errors he has permitted as a matter of historical fact and then fashion our ecclesiology accordingly.

PRACTICAL CONCLUSIONS

It is the business of our bishops to give pastoral directives in this matter. But while we are awaiting more specific instructions, I offer the following practical advice.

First, when acting in his official capacity as preacher, counselor or confessor a priest should state without ambiguity that it is at present the authentic non-infallible teaching of the magisterium that every contraceptive act is immoral. If he admits that his private opinion is different from the official one, he should make clear that his opinion is a personal one and that he is not setting himself up as a competing magisterium in conflict with a far more authoritative one. He owes it to those he is instructing or counseling not to subtly manipulate them in any way into choosing his dissenting view rather than the official teaching of the Church. It is possible for a priest to be paternalistic and make decisions of conscience for the faithful by clever manipulation as well as by crass authoritarianism. This would not only be an abuse of his office but a disservice to the people. It only perpetuates clerical paternalism and Christian heteronomy in a more subtle way. If the goal of a pastor's ministry is the personal growth and responsibility of the faithful and what he is after in his priesthood is not control over the consciences and thoughts of others, then he will simply aid them as fairly and honestly as he can in the formation of their own consciences. He will not make their decisions for them as if they were the children he himself does not have.

Secondly, if I am correct in saying that any informed and reflective lay person has a right to dissent from authoritative magisterial teaching, the priest must respect this right in the confessional and not make the theoretical or practical rejection of the Church's teaching sufficient cause for refusal of the sacraments. If the confessor is asked by the penitent about the morality of contraception, he should explain the official teaching of the Church and instruct the penitent about the rights and primacy of the individual conscience and of the ruthless honesty necessary in forming it. He should aid him as far as is necessary in forming his own sincere conscience and then respect his honest decision no matter what it is. If his honest decision of conscience is one of dissent from papal teaching, he should be told that he need not bring the matter of birth control up in the confessional before receiving the Eucharist.

Finally, even if a priest does not agree that any informed and reflective lay person has an objective right to dissent from authoritative papal teaching, he still must allow the individual to follow his conscience in this matter. Conscience is not formed deductively, by syllogistic reasoning such as: what the pope teaches is true; the pope teaches that contraception is evil; therefore it is true that contraception is evil. Conscience is formed by a personal appropriation of values and more than theoretical knowledge is necessary for this.

The important distinction drawn by modern psychiatry between theoretical and evaluative knowledge is described succinctly by Josef Fuchs:

Moral knowledge which is merely (more or less) theoretical is one thing; knowledge which is also evaluative is quite another. Only this latter is moral knowledge in the full sense of the word. For in it man not only *knows* what the law or moral norm is; nor is his knowledge of the *value* of the moral norm restricted to the theoretical type. But this knowledge of the law and its moral value he genuinely appropriates to himself, so that he is able to perceive and *evaluate* the goodness personally and concretely, even in such a way that this knowledge arouses a spiritual affection which flows over into the senses. Sometimes this evaluative cognition is absent, although the theoretical cognition remains. This absence is either *habitual* as may happen for example in pathological personalities or also in children (children of eight have perhaps well learned what actions are gravely sinful without being able to weigh sufficiently the value of a virtuous act and the concept of grave sin), or it is merely *actual*. This may happen, for example, because of habit or passion, in the moment of temptation if the value of the moral good is hardly any longer perceived and weighed.[12]

The knowledge requisite for a mortal sin is not merely theoretical or speculative. It must be evaluative or appreciative. A person must do more than know intellectually that a certain action is wrong. He must make this knowledge his own. He must personally perceive the moral good or evil involved in an action so that he evaluates or appreciates it emotionally as well as in a purely abstract way. He must experience a certain emotional or affective revulsion from the evil, so that he can be said to feel as well as know that it is wrong. If in any situation a person lacks evaluative or appreciative knowledge of this sort, or if he does not have it in sufficient intensity to elicit a fundamental option, he lacks the kind of knowledge that must be present for mortal sin.

Many Catholics are aware of the teaching of *Humanae Vitae* but for a variety of reasons are not able at the present time to appropriate as their own the values that it affirms. The pope's conscience does not automatically become their conscience. Even if the confessor does not admit our conclusion, that every individual has the objective right to dissent from papal teaching, still he must respect the subjective rights of conscience and absolve as a person in good faith anyone who cannot personally appropriate with evaluative knowledge the teaching of *Humanae Vitae*.

7. Divorce and Remarriage

ALTHOUGH THE understanding of marriage as an indissoluble monogamous union of a man and a woman is for all practical purposes a conception that is peculiar to the Catholic Church, some form of marriage as a socially regulated institution seems to have been the normal pattern in the history of homo sapiens. Twentieth-century diggings appear to have refuted the revolutionary theories of nineteenth-century anthropologists who thought that marriage evolved from stages of primitive promiscuity through group marriages and polygamy to monogamous marriage.

There has, of course, been a great deal of variety in the conception and practice of marriage in different cultures. Certain economic and social factors favored on certain occasions the development of polygamy and more rarely polyandry. In the primitive Manus society of New Guinea husbands are expected to hate their wives. In some Eskimo tribes husbands offer their wives to visitors as a sign of hospitality and courtesy. This thoughtful Eskimo practice appears to be catching on in certain more sophisticated tribes in contemporary North America where people like Bob and Carol and Ted and Alice are experimenting with wife-swapping and other young people are trying out communal societies in place of marriage.

On the whole, however, monogamous marriage of some sort seems to have been and is the rule and everything else an exception. Because overall social and economic conditions are so deeply affected, society generally has not regarded marriage as the private business of the two partners but has always shown an interest in regulating and controlling it. It is, however, only rarely that any society has controlled it with the inflexibility of the Catholic Church in demanding that it be *datis dandis* absolutely indissoluble.

SACRED SCRIPTURE

In the Old Testament monogamous permanent marriage was seen as the ideal throughout most of Israel's history (cf. Tob. 7:10–11 and 8:6–8; Wisdom literature passim; Gen. 2:18 and 23). It was an ideal of secular life shared by most of Israel's neighbors in the Near East. The institution of marriage was viewed as primarily for the preservation of the husband's clan rather than for the benefit of the marriage partners. Hence it is not surprising that for the good of the clan certain forms of polygamy and concubinage with slaves were allowed (cf. Exod. 21: 7–11; Deut. 21:10–15). For the good of the clan, marriage could be dissolved by the man because of barrenness, adultery or incompatibility. Although it was not specifically provided for by law, the wife also was usually able to get a divorce if she could no longer reasonably be expected to live with her husband.

The so-called divorce law of Deuteronomy 24: 1–4 stated that a man may divorce his wife if he "has found some impropriety of which to accuse her." All he had to do was hand her a writ of divorce stating that she is no longer his wife and then dismiss her from his house. What "some impropriety" means is not explained. This ambiguity later gave rise to the dispute between the schools of Rabbi Shammai and Rabbi Hillel. The former judged that adultery alone was sufficient grounds for divorce; the latter, interpreting the law more liberally and according to the actual practice, thought that many, even insignificant, reasons were sufficient grounds.

On the whole, however, the Old Testament

seems to have discouraged divorce (e.g., Deut. 22: 13–19 and 28–29). In Malachi 2:13–16 we read: "And here is something else you do: you cover the altar of Yahweh with tears, with weeping and wailing, because he now refuses to consider the offering or to accept it from your hands. And you ask, 'Why?' It is because Yahweh stands as witness between you and the wife of your youth, the wife with whom you have broken faith, even though she was your partner and your wife by covenant. Did he not create a single being that has flesh and the breath of life? And what is this single being destined for? God-given offspring. Be careful of your own life, therefore, and do not break faith with the wife of your youth. For I hate divorce, says Yahweh the God of Israel. . . ."

It is not likely, however, that this condemnation was as sweeping as it sounds. It was directed to those Jews who were divorcing their Israelite wives to marry the daughters of pagan soldiers. Schillebeeckx comments that this seems to have been a kind of "privilege of faith" working in the opposite direction.[1]

In the New Testament both the synoptic gospels and Paul indicate that on at least one occasion Jesus rejected divorce in principle. The exact saying of Jesus is unknown. There seem to be two traditions or sources, one Marcan, from which Mark 10:11–12 and Matthew 19:9 are derived, and the other Q, from which Luke 16:18 and Matthew 5:32 come. Paul's rewording of the teaching in 1 Corinthians 7:10–11 is so much his own that its source cannot be traced.

The Q form is generally believed to be the most primitive. Luke groups three independent sayings of Jesus together; the third is this: "Everyone who divorces his wife and marries another is guilty of adultery, and the man who marries a woman divorced by her husband commits adultery" (Luke 16:18). Matthew took the same logion which appeared in Q without any narrative context and inserted it into his account of the Sermon on the Mount: "It has also been said: *Anyone who divorces his wife must give her a writ of dismissal.* But I say this to you: everyone who divorces his wife, except for the case of fornication, makes her an adulteress; and anyone who marries a divorced woman commits adultery" (Matt. 5:31–32).

Mark places the saying as he found it in the context of a conflict situation with the Pharisees:

> Some Pharisees approached him and asked, "Is it against the law for a man to divorce his wife?" They were testing him. He answered them, "What did Moses command you?" "Moses allowed us," they said, "to draw up a writ of dismissal and so to divorce." Then Jesus said to them, "It was because you were so unteachable

that he wrote this commandment for you. But from the beginning of creation *God made them male and female. This is why a man must leave father and mother, and the two become one body.* They are no longer two, therefore, but one body. So then, what God has united, man must not divide." Back in the house the disciples questioned him again about this, and he said to them, "The man who divorces his wife and marries another is guilty of adultery against her. And if a woman divorces her husband and marries another she is guilty of adultery too" (Mark 10:2–12).

Matthew's parallel rendition seems to fit better into the Palestinian context, since in his report he does not take into account the possibility of a wife divorcing her husband:

Some Pharisees approached him, and to test him they said, "Is it against the Law for a man to divorce his wife on any pretext whatever?" He answered, "Have you not read that the creator from the beginning *made them male and female* and that he said: *This is why a man must leave father and mother, and cling to his wife, and the two become one body?* They are no longer two, therefore, but one body. So then, what God has united, man must not divide." They said to him, "Then why did Moses command that a writ of dismissal should be given in cases of divorce?" "It was because you were so unteachable," he said, "that Moses allowed you to divorce your wives,

but it was not like this from the beginning. Now
I say this to you: the man who divorces his wife
—I am not speaking of fornication—and marries
another, is guilty of adultery" (Matt. 19:3-9).

St. Paul testifies to the existence of this teaching
from Jesus when he writes in 1 Corinthians 7:10–11:
"For the married I have something to say, and this
is not from me but from the Lord: a wife must not
leave her husband—or if she does leave him, she
must either remain unmarried or else make it up
with her husband—nor must a husband send his
wife away."

The principal difference between Matthew and
the others is that in the latter Jesus is reported as
having rejected divorce absolutely, while Matthew
appears to make an exception—"expect for *porneia*."
More than a dozen explanations of this clause have
been offered in recent years. All of them have some
likelihood, but the one that appears least likely to
exegetes today is the one that translates *porneia* as
adultery, as if Matthew is suggesting that in the
mind of Jesus adultery may be legitimate grounds
for divorce. In a paper delivered to the Catholic
Theological Society in 1967, Bruce Vawter remarked:
"If, as is facilely taken for granted by so many com-
mentators, Matthew's redactions were a New Testament attempt to soften the rigidity of a primitive
Christian discipline and reduce it to 'practical' lim-

its, it was an attempt that singularly failed, if we may judge from the literature and practice of the subapostolic Church which—generally—recognized no such mitigation to have taken place."[2]

The question, of course, can be argued and has been argued for centuries. In the light of present-day knowledge and contemporary exegesis it seems fair to say that the best conclusion we can draw is that Jesus' teaching on divorce was truly radical and revolutionary: he rejected all divorce in principle and did not make an exception for adultery or anything else.

If we accept this conclusion, we still have another question to ask about the normative value of his teaching. One may assume that he replaced the divorce law of Deuteronomy with a new more radical law for the New Testament which expresses the eternal, immutable will of God for all men and that fulfillment of this new law is now made possible for men by the superabundant grace of the Redemption. If this assumption is correct, then the *Code of Canon Law* is correct when it states: "Marriage which is *ratum et consummatum* cannot be dissolved by any human power nor by any cause save death."[3] But there is another possibility.

Vawter believes that the context in which Matthew first inserts Jesus' logion, namely the Sermon on the Mount, is most significant in evaluating its normative character. Here Jesus is not replacing imperfect legislation with new legislation which is now the measure of a Christian's righteousness. Nor is he merely giving optional directives or counsels of perfection. He is giving true commands addressed to the Christian conscience; but these commands are not legal rules but normative ideals or goals. They are ideals which we must strive to realize even though it will not always be possible. We will always have to make adaptations in impossible situations but that does not mean that the commands are merely beautiful but unrealizable ideals. They remain true commands prescribing an ideal that is binding and possible.

Accordingly, Jesus' command regarding divorce was not the promulgation of a divine law. It was the call to an ideal which is addressed to and binding on the Christian conscience. But the Christian conscience will always be faced with situations in which this ideal cannot be realized.

TRADITION

A recent study made by Anthony Bevilacqua shows that in the history of the Church a number of adaptations or compromises have occurred.[4]

Although the text is obscure and nothing certain can be concluded, it seems that in his *Divine Institutions,* written about 305–310, Lactantius permits an innocent husband to divorce his wife on account of adultery and to remarry. Ambrosiaster, a little known ecclesiastical writer commenting around 370–375 on 1 Corinthians 7:10–11, clearly permits a husband, but not a wife, to remarry after divorce. Some historians claim that Pope St. Gregory II (715–731) permitted remarriage after divorce, but the text offered as proof is ambiguous.

There are also indications of compromise in some local ecclesiastical councils and synods. The Second Synod of St. Patrick, which appears to be a collection of replies to various questions rather than a true synod, seems to permit an innocent man to remarry after divorcing his wife for adultery. The manuscript, however, is corrupt and not easy to decipher. In the Councils of Verberies (753) and Compiègne (756) Church leaders appear to have accommodated their teaching to the Frankish secular law permitting divorce and remarriage in certain circumstances. The Council of Rome (826) under Pope Eugenius II and the Council of Bourges (1031) make at least ambiguous statements about divorce and remarriage in the case of adultery.

The penitential books of the seventh and eighth centuries permitted divorce and remarriage for a number of reasons, such as mutual consent, change of status from freeman to slave and vice versa, captivity, infirmity, impotence, adultery, abandonment by a wife for two to five years and entrance into religious life. These books were written by individual priests and had no official authority, but they were widely used by confessors in the Celtic and Anglo-Saxon lands and so reflect the local practice of that time.

These few instances, however, are exceptions and not the rule. Bevilacqua's study shows that in the West from the second to the tenth century the Fathers, Roman Pontiffs, Church councils and synods made no compromise with secular law and practice. Their teaching was practically unanimous: no divorce and remarriage; Christian marriage can be dissolved only by death. The same rigidity was found in the Eastern Church until about the sixth century. At that time, under the influence of secular law and practice, the Christian practice gradually grew more lax, although for a while the official teaching remained the same. Eventually, however, Church teaching in the East was accommodated to the prevailing practice.

It is important to note that the Catholic doctrine of indissolubility was taught at the Council of Trent but the Church Fathers were careful not to define it as dogma since they did not want on that occasion to condemn the Greeks as heretics. In reiterating the Catholic doctrine of indissolubility in *Casti Connubii* Pope Pius XI said only that this doctrine is certain but not that it is defined.[5]

THE THEOLOGICAL ARGUMENT

Theologians and canonists hold that the Roman Pontiff can grant not only annulments but in certain circumstances divorces of valid marriages with the right to remarry. He can dissolve not only valid non-consummated marriages but also valid consummated marriages when at least one of the parties is not validly baptized, even if the marriage took place in the Catholic Church with the requisite dispensation from the impediment of disparity of cult and according to the proper canonical form, i.e., before a priest and two witnesses. The only marriage that the pope cannot dissolve, they argue, is a valid consummated marriage between two baptized persons, whether contracted in or outside the Church.

The natural law arguments for the indissolubility of marriage, therefore, are not judged to lead to any absolute conclusion. The good of the children, of the couples or of society are relative not absolute goods which may in certain circumstances be better provided for by divorce and remarriage; or they may represent values which can be sacrificed in certain cases for the sake of a more important value, as occurs when valid marriages are dissolved by the Holy Father "in favor of the faith."

The fundamental argument, therefore, for the absolute indissolubility of Christian marriage *ratum et consummatum* derives not from human reason but from St. Paul's teaching in Ephesians 5:21–33:

> Wives should regard their husbands as they regard the Lord, since as Christ is head of the Church and saves the whole body, so is a husband the head of his wife; and as the Church submits to Christ, so should wives to their husbands, in everything. Husbands should love their wives just as Christ loved the Church and sacrificed himself for her to make her holy. He made her clean by washing her in water with a form of words, so that when he took her to himself she would be glorious, with no speck or wrinkle or anything like that, but holy and faultless. In the same way, husbands must love their wives as they love their own bodies; for a man to love his wife is for him to love himself. A man never hates his own body, but he feeds it and looks after it; and that is the way Christ treats the Church, because it is his body—and we are its living parts. *For this reason, a man must leave his father and mother and be joined to his wife, and the two will become one body*. This mystery has many implications; but I am saying it applies to Christ and the Church.

The theological argument based on this text is that the sacrament of matrimony, which is given only to baptized Christians, is a special sign of the union of Christ with his Church. His union with his Church is permanent: he is absolutely inseparable from it and will never abandon it. Christian marriage, therefore, as a sign of this indissoluble union is itself indissoluble.

There is no doubt that this is the understanding of Christian marriage that Paul had in mind. It is an inspiring and challenging description of Christian love and Christian marriage and it explains why Christian marriage is indissoluble. But, as we have noted above, the question remains: Is its indissolubility a normative ideal or a legal precept? There is no reason to prove that this argument is any more conclusive than the former.

PRACTICAL CONCLUSIONS

There has been little serious discussion about the traditional teaching of the Church on divorce, but questions are now beginning to be raised and I suspect that in the near future they will receive the attention and study of scholars that they deserve. Whether this study can be carried on without the sensationalism that attended the birth control argument is questionable. In any event, one should be careful not to offer people prematurely the cruel comfort of false hopes.

In our swiftly changing world predictions are dangerous. However, I do not expect that the Catholic Church will suddenly reverse her teaching on divorce and remarriage. What we might more realistically look for is a better understanding of marriage and changes in canon law. Some possibilities are a clearer understanding of the marriage contract and perhaps a less biological view of the meaning of consummation, juridical presumption in favor of freedom rather than in favor of the marriage bond, a wider understanding and acceptance of psychic impotence as a diriment impediment, the decentralization of matrimonial decisions and a greater extension of good faith cases.[6]

I suspect that every reader knows a Catholic now living in an invalid marriage because of a previous marriage of one of the partners. Many of these people feel deeply the pain of not being able to receive the sacraments and wish that something could be done about their situation. If something is going to be done about the majority of these cases, at least in the near future, the single most important factor will not be a change in the *Code of Canon Law*. The single most important factor will be the knowledge and interest of the parish priest.

When I first arrived from parish work to teach moral theology I began the first class with a rather nervous explanation of the importance of the study of moral theology. A rather unnervous student asked me what was the most practical subject I had studied in the seminary, what subject I actually used most in the parish. With hardly any reflection I dropped the case I was making for moral theology and answered, "Canon law." Let me explain this strange reply.

If a priest takes a census in his parish not merely to gather information on a set of file cards but as an excuse to ring every doorbell in the parish in order to bring his ministry to every person in the parish, he will find on almost every block some Catholic who is not registered as a parishioner, is not going to church, has not had the children baptized or instructed and is very unhappy and depressed about it all. There will be various reasons, but the most common one will be an invalid marriage because one of the partners had been married before, got divorced and remarried outside the Church. Most of these people will say that they wanted to be married in the Church but a priest told them that nothing could be done. It is a conservative estimate to say that in at least one-half of the cases something can be done but was not done because of a priest's indifference or laziness, or more often because of his simple ignorance of canon law.

The *Code of Canon Law* is now fifty years old. It was already somewhat quaint at the time of its original promulgation, so it is no surprise that much of it is outmoded and needs revision. But while — waiting for a new code, which also will be somewhat quaint, a pastor who is committed to living in an imperfect Church as well as in an imperfect world will know the law and how to use it for the good of his people. He will be alert to all the possibilities of having the first marriage declared null by the ecclesiastical courts: the Catholic baptism of one of the parties in the first marriage and the consequent lack of canonical form, the absence or invalidity of the baptism of either party in the first marriage, a previous bond, defective consent, the presence of some diriment impediment and so forth. Surprisingly, something that is sometimes overlooked is the matter of death. People do die and an investigation will sometimes reveal that one of those who has died is the former husband or wife. Even if one of the present marriage partners is not willing to cooperate in having the marriage validated, the canonically sophisticated pastor will know how to petition and get a *sanatio in radice*. It is not easy to sympathize with those priests who dismiss all this as juridical "Mickey Mouse" when one sees how important it is to many people that they have their marriage validated by the Church and be allowed to return to the sacraments.

Pastoral zeal and legal knowledge, however, will not be enough to solve all the agonizing cases that occur. There will always remain the painful legally insoluble situations of good people who made a mistake in the past, which was not always their fault, and who are now divorced, living in a second marriage, love one another, are leading exemplary Christian lives and are raising their children to be vital members of Christ's Church. Some of them lie awake at night worrying about their condition and yet do not feel that they can break up their homes and families and go off to live separately.

Three moralists, B. Peters, T. Beemer and C. van der Poel, published an interesting article entitled "Cohabitation in a 'Marital State of Mind.' "[7] According to the authors, those who cohabit in a "marital state of mind" are those invalidly married couples for whom there is no juridical solution and who in the circumstances have no other practical option than cohabitation. They "consider themselves married to each other" and "possess the mental and emotional dispositions which are proper to marriage itself," as well as being responsible for their children. These people, the authors argue, might be allowed to receive the sacraments even though their marriage cannot be legally rectified.

Commenting on this contribution to the resolution of a difficult pastoral problem, Richard Mc-Cormick wrote:

It is easy to agree with Peters, Beemer, and van der Poel that the "marital state of mind," the willingness to educate the children, and the desire for sacramental participation are assuredly important aspects of the situation. They must not be forgotten. But they are not the only aspects. There is always the danger that a one-sided emphasis of these aspects could lead both priest and couple to view the present impasse as a juridical mistake of the past only. However, the past sacramental and consummated but broken marriage is not simply a matter of the past; it is, if our doctrine on divorce and remarriage means anything, as unavoidably a part of the *present* situation as the mature affection and the "marital state of mind." Here and now at least one of these [partners] is irrevocably given to another. To allow the "marital state of mind" to obscure this fact or mitigate its demands is to analyze the present situation in terms of only one of its existential aspects. The present situation is not only a state of mind; it is also a state of persons.[8]

McCormick does not deny but asserts that "the possibility that these trapped and suffering individuals could approach the sacraments is a question which can be legitimately asked." But he thinks that "before one can answer the question about the sacraments, he must be clear on the moral status of these relationships, that is, that such couples are not truly husband and wife. Otherwise compassion and confusion will have become pastoral companions."

I think that this is a reasonable caution. With it in mind let us ask the question straightforwardly: May invalidly married couples receive the sacraments? I think that there are three possible approaches to this practical problem.

One is to give the expected and customary answer, and in fact the answer that McCormick gives: no, not as long as they continue to cohabit in an invalid marriage. If this approach is taken, it is very important how it is understood and explained. Participation in the Eucharist is an objective sign of unity with the ecclesial community. The objective condition of a divorced and remarried person is a visible pattern of life at odds with the ecclesial community and its beliefs about marriage. There is, therefore, an external objective conflict between the sign-dimensions of the sacraments and the social conduct. The fundamental reason, therefore, why he may not receive the sacraments is that their reception would be an objective external falsification of the significance of the sacrament. The reason is not because he is living in sin. No judgment is made or implied about his personal moral condition. He may well be living in God's grace as much as anyone else, and as much as anyone else he has the obligation to continue all his efforts to live close to God, even though this one access through the sacraments is closed to him for external reasons.[9]

Another possible approach is the *frater-soror* (brother-sister) arrangement. It is obvious that this is not the solution to all difficult cases, but it would be a mistake to think a priori that it is a viable solution only for old people who have lost interest in sex. It is not sufficient to dismiss this as a possibility because it is unreal and does not work. It does not have to work. Only a legalistic mind thinks it does. All that is required is that one have the prevailing intention to make it work. After he receives permission to live in a brother-sister relationship, one is in the same position as anyone living in a necessary occasion of sin. He may fall a great number of times despite a serious and sincere intention, but at least he has access to the sacraments, which may be a very important source of comfort and help to him as he struggles to live his day-to-day life. I do not want to overplay this as a solution, nor do I mean to encourage any kind of insincerity, but I do want to caution against any doctrinaire rejection of this approach as if it is never worthy of serious consideration. In some situations it will provide the best relief of intolerable anguish.

The third possible approach is suggested by Karl Rahner in *The Christian Commitment:*

> A man's ability genuinely and existentially to grasp particular values (which is a necessary condition for subjectively grave sin) is very largely

he product of his environment. We cannot countenance any departure from the objective moral norm. But our proclamation of Christian principles ought not to ignore the fact that there are not only in individual cases *causae excusantes a peccato formali* but, among Catholics living in the diaspora, general sociological causes: a hardness of heart which is socially conditioned and generally present. Have we asked ourselves searchingly enough what follows from this?—not indeed as regards moral norms, but as regards our practical pastoral attitude. . . . What, for instance, am I to do with a Catholic whose second "marriage" (invalid because of the divorce of one party) has been of moral benefit to him, because he does not see this second marriage as immoral, on account of his socially, culturally, historically conditioned hardness of heart . . . and its consequences for him, morally as well as in other ways, have been entirely happy? We are not going to assume, *a priori,* that in questions of this sort all further thought on more practically useful methods of applying general principles is bound to be entirely superfluous.[10]

I am not sure whether I am reading it into or out of Rahner's text, but what I think he is hinting at is the possibility of an application of the moral doctrine on the kind of evaluative knowledge necessary for a fundamental option.[11] If a divorced person living in a second marriage finds himself not only unable to meet but even to understand an obligation to dissolve his present marriage with all the painful consequences for the children and for the couple themselves, and he truly cannot accept such a demand as being the binding will of God for him —if, in other words, he cannot truly feel that this marriage is immoral but rather feels that the real immorality would be its dissolution—does it not follow that he has a personal obligation to remain in the present union and not to break it up? And does it not further follow that he is therefore not sinning personally but is living in God's grace? If so, does he not have a right to the sacraments as long as there is no public knowledge of his condition and so no public scandal and harm to the Church?

I think that this solution deserves serious consideration, although it is not without its problems. Perhaps one could argue that if it became common practice public scandal and the external falsification of the significance of the sacraments would inevitably result. Or, perhaps, to guard against these dangers the bishop of a diocese would want to reserve such permissions to himself. Whatever the case, I think it is a question worth asking.

Notes

CHAPTER 1

1. Rollo May, *Love and Will* (New York: W. W. Norton & Co., 1969).

2. Alfred C. Kinsey et al., *Sexual Behavior in the Human Female* (Philadelphia: W. B. Saunders Co., 1953), p. 660.

3. May, *Love and Will*, pp. 113–114.

4. A number of good manuals are available. Three of the best are: James Leslie McCary, *Human Sexuality* (New York: D. Van Nostrand Co., 1967); Karl Wrage, *Man and Woman* (Philadelphia: Fortress Press, 1969); and Theodor H. Van de Velde, *Ideal Marriage* (New York: Covici, Friede, 1930).

5. William H. Masters and Virginia E. Johnson, *Human Sexual Response* (Boston: Little, Brown & Co., 1966).

6. May, *Love and Will*, p. 38.

Notes

CHAPTER 2

1. Vance Packard, *The Sexual Wilderness* (New York: David McKay Co., 1968).

2. Kinsey, *Sexual Behavior in the Human Female*, pp. 228–231.

3. Before *Eros* magazine went out of existence its pages considered this weighty question: "How do porcupines do it?" The answer, of course, was: "Carefully."

4. DS 835. (H. Denzinger, *Enchiridion Symbolorum*, ed. Adolf Schönmetzer; Freiburg, 1965).

5. DS 897.

6. DS 899.

7. DS 1367.

8. DS 2045.

9. DS 2148.

10. DS 3706.

11. DS 2060.

12. Josef Fuchs, S.J., *De Castitate et Ordine Sexuali* (Rome: Gregorian University, 1960), p. 111.

13. A. Vermeersch, S.J., *De Castitate* (Rome: Gregorian University, 1921), p. 341.

14. *Archivo Teológico Granadino* 23 (1960): 5–138.

15. Fuchs, *De Castitate et Ordine Sexuali*, p. 35.

16. Paul Ramsey, "A Christian Approach to the Question of Sexual Relations Outside of Marriage," *The Journal of Religion* 45 (1965): 100–118.

17. *Theological Studies* 26 (1965) : 625–626.

18. Peter A. Bertocci, *Sex, Love, and the Person* (New York: Sheed and Ward, 1967).

19. See Fuchs, *De Castitate et Ordine Sexuali,* p. 111.

CHAPTER 3

1. See L. Dearborn, "Masturbation," in *Encyclopedia of Sexual Behavior* (New York: Hawthorn Books, 1947).

2. Kinsey, *Sexual Behavior in the Human Female* and *Sexual Behavior in the Human Male* (Philadelphia: W. B. Saunders Co., 1948).

3. Masters and Johnson, *Human Sexual Response,* p. 63.

4. McCary, *Human Sexuality,* p. 292.

5. DS 688.

6. *Religiosorum institutio,* no. 30.

7. DS 2044.

8. DS 2149.

9. Reprinted in M. Zalba, S.J., *Theologiae Moralis Summa,* vol. 2 (Madrid: Biblioteca de Autores Cristianos, 1957), p. 160, note 39.

10. DS 3684.

11. Cf. Pius XII, *Acta Apostolicae Sedis* 48 (1956), 472.

'2. *AAS* 44 (1952), 275.

Notes

13. John C. Ford, S.J., and Gerald Kelly, S.J., *Contemporary Moral Theology,* vol. 1 (Westminster, Md.: The Newman Press, 1958), pp. 175–176.

14. *AAS* 53 (1961), 571.

15. Fuchs, *De Castitate et Ordine Sexuali,* p. 50.

16. Unpublished notes on "Christian Chastity for the Unmarried," 1968, p. 60.

17. Henri Gibert, *Love in Marriage* (New York: Hawthorn Books, 1964), pp. 172–173.

18. Charles Curran, "Masturbation and Objectively Grave Matter: An Exploratory Discussion," *Proceedings* 21 (1966): 95–109.

19. Ibid., p. 106.

20. Josef Fuchs, S.J., *Theologia Moralis Generalis,* vol. 2 (Rome: Gregorian University, 1966), pp. 131–169; P. Schoonenberg, S.J., *Man and Sin* (Notre Dame, Ind.: The University of Notre Dame Press, 1965).

21. Conversely, in estimating the gravity of matter one must be careful not to be unilaterally objectve. Grave matter is that which can found a presumption of a fundamental option.

CHAPTER 4

1. E. Schillebeeckx, O.P., *Celibacy* (New York: Sheed and Ward, 1968), p. 76.

2. *Lumen Gentium,* nos. 40 and 42.

Notes

3. Quentin Quesnell, S.J., " 'Made themselves eunuchs for the kingdom of heaven' (Mt. 19:12)," *Theology Digest* 17 (1969) : 222–226. Originally published in the *Catholic Biblical Quarterly* 30 (1968) : 335–358. J. Dupont, O.S.B., *Mariage et Divorce dans L'Évangile: Matthieu 19:3–12 et Parallèles.* (Bruges: Abbaye de saint André, 1959).

4. See, for instance, the recent contributions of Schillebeeckx, Rahner, Häring, Oraison and Auer.

5. Karl Rahner, S.J., "Der Zölibat des Weltpriesters im heutigen Gespräch," in *Geist und Leben* 40 (1967) : 122–138.

6. Bernard Häring, C.Ss.R., "Le célibat sacerdotal," in *Documentation catholique* 64 (1967) : 863.

7. Richard McCormick, S.J., "Notes on Moral Theology," *Theological Studies* 28 (1967): 782–783.

CHAPTER 5

1. See Richard H. Niebuhr, *The Responsible Self* (New York: Harper & Row, 1963).

2. Immanuel Kant, "On a Supposed Right to Lie from Altruistic Motives," in *Critique of Practical Reason and Other Writings in Moral Philosophy* (Chicago: University of Chicago Press, 1949).

3. Paul Ramsey, "Moral and Religious Implications of Genetic Control," in *Genetics and the Future of Man* (New York: Appleton-Century-Crofts, 1965).

167

Notes

4. I am passing over the topic of abortion, since it has its own peculiar problems and its consideration here would enlarge our discussion beyond any workable limits. I might mention in passing that the "morning after" pill, which is now in the research stage, is an abortifacient, not simply a contraceptive.

5. In addition to the works listed in note 4 to chapter 1, see Lawrence Q. Crawley et al., *Reproduction, Sex, and Preparation for Marriage* (Englewood Cliffs, N.J.: Prentice-Hall, 1964).

6. Cf. the discussion on this point in McCormick, "Notes," *Theological Studies* 27 (1966): 646.

7. To the delight of many pet owners it is equally effective in cats and dogs.

8. Pills which cause temporary sterility in men are still in the experimental or research stage.

9. Because it is so complicated I am not surprised that I have encountered women who had gotten the whole thing backwards and so had frequent intercourse during the fertile period and abstained heroically during the rest of the month.

10. Address to Planned Parenthood Affiliates, May 15, 1962.

11. Other techniques sometimes used are for all practical purposes ineffective.

12. *Theological Studies* 29 (1968): 737.

13. Fuchs, *Theologia Moralis Generalis,* p. 45.

14. *Humanae Vitae,* no. 12.

15. Ramsey, "A Christian Approach to the Question of Sexual Relations Outside of Marriage."

16. Fuchs, *Theologia Moralis Generalis,* p. 80.

CHAPTER 6

1. Reprinted in Robert Hoyt, ed., *The Birth Control Debate* (Kansas City: *National Catholic Reporter*, 1968).

2. Ibid.

3. *Dignitatis Humanae,* no. 14.

4. *Lumen Gentium,* no. 25.

5. *Praestantia,* DS 3503.

6. G. Van Noort, *Dogmatic Theology,* vol. 3 (Westminster, Md.: The Newman Press, 1961), p. 272.

7. *Theological Studies* 30 (1969): 643–644.

8. *Theological Studies* 29 (1968): 737.

9. Ford and Kelly, *Contemporary Moral Theology,* vol. 2 (Westminster, Md.: The Newman Press, 1963), p. 258.

10. John T. Noonan, Jr., *Contraception* (New York: New American Library, 1967).

11. B. Schüller, S.J., "Remarks on the Authentic Pronouncements of the Magisterium," *Theology Digest* 16 (1968): 331.

12. Josef Fuchs, S.J., *Theologia Moralis Generalis,* vol. 1 (Rome: Gregorian University, 1963), pp. 155–156.

CHAPTER 7

1. E. Schillebeeckx, O.P., *Marriage: Human Reality and Saving Mystery* (New York: Sheed and Ward, 1965), p. 94.

Notes

2. Bruce Vawter, C.M., "The Biblical Theology of Divorce," *Proceedings* 22 (1967): 223–244.

3. C. 1118.

4. A. Bevilacqua, "The History of the Indissolubility of Marriage," *Proceedings* 22 (1967): 253–308.

5. *Casti Connubii,* no. 89.

6. See the interesting contribution made at a symposium sponsored by the Canon Law Society: W. Bassett, ed., *The Bond of Marriage* (Notre Dame, Ind.: The University of Notre Dame Press, 1968).

7. *Homiletic and Pastoral Review* 66 (1966): 566–577.

8. *Theological Studies* 27 (1966): 623–624.

9. See M. Huftier, "Sur la séparation de divorcés remaries," in *Ami du clergé* 76 (1966): 201–207.

10. Karl Rahner, *The Christian Commitment* (New York: Sheed and Ward, 1963), pp. 31–32.

11. See chapter 6.